Ethics
and the Early Childhood Educator

Using the NAEYC Code
Second Edition

Stephanie Feeney and Nancy K. Freeman,
with Peter J. Pizzolongo

National Association for the Education of Young Children
Washington, D.C.

National Association for the
Education of Young Children
1313 L Street NW, Suite 500
Washington, DC 20005-4101
202-232-8777 • 800-424-2460
www.naeyc.org

NAEYC Books

Chief Publishing Officer
Derry Koralek

Editor-in-Chief
Kathy Charner

Director of Creative Services
Edwin C. Malstrom

Senior Editor
Holly Bohart

Design and Production
Malini Dominey

Assistant Editor
Elizabeth Wegner

Editorial Assistant
Ryan Smith

Contributing editors: *Lacy Thompson* and *Steve Olle*

**Ethics and the Early Childhood Educator:
Using the NAEYC Code, Second Edition**

Library of Congress Control Number: 2012938435
ISBN: 978-1-928896-83-8
NAEYC Item #368

Acknowledgments

This book is intended to help early childhood educators learn about ethics and about the NAEYC Code of Ethical Conduct and how it can be applied in work with young children and their families. It rests on a strong foundation of ethical theory and NAEYC's more than 20 years of work on professional ethics.

We would like to express our deep appreciation to the following:

Lilian Katz for her pioneering work on professional ethics in early childhood education and her consultation on the first edition of this book.

Kenneth Kipnis, whose expertise continues to enhance our understanding of professional ethics. Ideas for both editions of this book have been influenced by his writing and our ongoing conversations with him.

Marilyn Smith, former executive director of NAEYC, who from the beginning enthusiastically supported the Association's work on ethics. We are very grateful for her support and the legacy it has created in the Association.

Those who served on the **NAEYC Panel on Professional Ethics** for the contributions they made to the Code's visibility during the formative years of work on ethics in early childhood education.

Eva Moravcik, Linda Newman, Mac Brown, and **Terry Haney** for helping us to conceptualize the first edition of this book.

Peter Pizzolongo, NAEYC associate executive director, for championing and participating in work on professional ethics and for his contributions to this second edition of *Ethics and the Early Childhood Educator.*

Derry Koralek, Lacy Thompson, and **Ryan Smith** for their thoughtful contributions to the editing of this book.

Wenjia Wang and **Francie Kneece,** Nancy's graduate assistants, for research and logistical support.

Our families—our husbands, Don Mickey and John Freeman, and Nancy's daughters, Gretchen and Nora, for their interest, encouragement, and contributions to this project.

Contents

Ideals: Knowledge and skills teachers should bring to work
Principles: rules
Core Values: Standards

Foreword to the Second Edition

The second edition of *Ethics and the Early Childhood Educator: Using the NAEYC Code* is an NAEYC resource that we are pleased to publish and that follows a history of two minor revisions to the first edition. This edition includes situations that involve ethical dimensions—responsibilities and dilemmas—based on the 2005 revision and the 2011 reaffirmation and updating of the Code.

In the April 2005 revision of the Code of Ethical Conduct and Statement of Commitment, and the 2011 reaffirmation and updating, NAEYC addressed issues that surfaced at the start of the twenty-first century and reflected language that has changed since the Code was revised in 1997. However, the 2005 and 2011 iterations of the Code presented an interesting dilemma. What should NAEYC do about its two books that supplement the Code (this one, and *Teaching the NAEYC Code of Ethical Conduct: Activity Sourcebook*)?

Typically, it is not possible to instantly update a whole book as NAEYC develops or updates position statements and resources. However, following the 2005 revision and 2011 updating, Stephanie Feeney and Nancy Freeman were able to work with us to prepare a modestly revised version of this text to include the 2005 Code revision. In 2011, they helped prepare a version of the book to address that updating of the position statement, which reflected consistency with the Supplement for Early Childhood Program Administrators (2006), and to ensure alignment with current best practices for family engagement. In these revised versions, the text addressing the Core Values, Ideals, and Principles was consistent with the 2005 and 2011 Codes. Modifications also focused on other matters that could be addressed with a "quick fix." However, the situations with ethical dimensions used as the cases in Chapters 4 through 7 did not include the new and modified Core Values, Ideals, and Principles.

This new edition of the book fully addresses the changes to the Code made in 2005 and 2011. It reflects current thinking on the value of addressing ethical issues in early childhood education and the situations with ethical dimensions fully represent the Core Values, Ideals, and Principles of the most current version of the Code.

I am quite fortunate to have had the privilege and pleasure of working with Stephanie, Nancy, and other NAEYC members and staff colleagues who participated in the revision and updating of the Code, as well as the publication of this text. I hope you find this book helpful in your work with children, families, and colleagues.

—*Peter J. Pizzolongo*

Foreword to the First Edition

Ethics—in the form of knowledge and skill in making responsible professional decisions—is one of the most fundamental qualities of a competent early childhood educator. Yet most teachers of young children, listing topics they want help on, would not put ethics at the top of their list. Topics more likely to appear high on their list include discipline, reading, parent collaboration, bilingual education, violence prevention, testing, and so on.

Ironically, these very topics are plagued with dilemmas for which NAEYC's Code of Ethical Conduct provides guidance for decision making. Herein lies a major challenge for achieving significant improvements in the practice of early childhood education: helping teachers grasp the potential help within the Code and dedicate effort to the study of these complex, yet powerful, tools to guide their decision making.

Stephanie Feeney and Nancy Freeman's work, *Ethics and the Early Childhood Educator: Using the NAEYC Code of Ethics,* meets this challenge head-on by contributing clearly stated concepts and examples as well as thought-provoking questions to guide the reader's exploration into the values and ethics that influence their professional decisions.

More and more early childhood professionals are exerting their leadership to promote increased understanding and application of NAEYC's Code of Ethical Conduct. Reflection on some of the barriers that hamper serious study of ethics could inform the steps we take to stimulate such investigation. Among the barriers that hamper the serious study of ethics are

- a tendency to view ethics as something inherent within us and thus not a quality that requires study or improvement;

- a belief that *right* and *wrong* are clearly defined and yield prescriptive rules and practices, thus contemplation is not required, just the discipline to do the right thing; and

- a disposition to settle for currently popular or comfortable solutions rather than face the daunting task of taking into account the multiple dynamics in the early childhood environment to individualize decisions for each child and situation.

Any or all of these barriers may arise for early childhood educators. Thus all efforts to engage them in exploring the role of ethics in their work should prompt individuals to begin with a careful examination of their currently held beliefs about ethics and morality.

Feeney and Freeman present a thoughtful framework for such explorations and use these insights to help the reader recognize the value of guiding principles from the Code of Ethical Conduct that have been generated from the combined wisdom and expertise of the early childhood field (see especially Chapter 1). They also show how NAEYC's Code blends standards for guidance with a process that allows for individualization.

The goal of NAEYC's Code of Ethical Conduct is to inform, not prescribe, answers in tough decisions that teachers and other early childhood professionals must make as they work with children and families. The strategy inherent in the Code is to promote the application of core values, ideals, and principles to guide decision making about ethical issues. This strategy is based on the belief that the early childhood educator is a dynamic, thinking individual and not a mechanistic robot whose actions are best controlled by penalties or rewards for producing specific behaviors prescribed by her or his professional organization or employer.

In the words of James L. Hymes Jr. (1983), a former president of NAEYC, "Young children need teachers who are not machines, not simply memories. They need people with searching hearts and seeking minds, people who are always trying better to understand themselves, their job, their young charges, and the world around them."

The story of how a code of ethics was developed for our profession presents an important reminder about how much can be accomplished through the leadership of a few people. In the mid-1970s, Evangeline Ward (1977), having just completed four years of service as president of NAEYC, began challenging NAEYC to assume leadership for developing a code of ethics for the field of early childhood education. In the style of great leaders, she had taken responsibility for drafting an initial code to stimulate debate before challenging others to take responsibility and get involved.

Simultaneously, Lilian Katz (1978) was encouraging discussion about the need for our field to develop a code by delineating some of the unique aspects of ethical issues in the practice of early childhood education and the contribution that could be made by a code of ethics. NAEYC published these works of Katz and Ward (1978), then in 1984 appointed a commission to develop a code of ethics. Stephanie Feeney was asked to chair this initiative and for the next five years devoted intense study to codes of ethics and led the Ethics Commission in crafting a code for our field. Lilian Katz participated in this work, as would have Evangeline Ward if not for her untimely death in 1985.

This story of the influence of these three women is not complete without noting these key aspects in their strategy: first, they devoted an extraordinary amount of study and thought to the ideas and proposals they put out for discussion; second, they were motivated by their commitment to advance their chosen profession; and third, they sought and valued ideas and suggestions from others, understanding that the final code would be enhanced from rigorous critique and that implementation would be more successful if familiarity and consensus had been built from many leaders in the field.

More than a decade has passed since NAEYC's Code of Ethical Conduct was adopted. During this period, attention to the importance of ethics in early childhood education has increased significantly. Chapter 8 of this book describes the numerous activities that are building early childhood educators' awareness of the Code and helping them learn to use the Code's core values, ideals, and principles to facilitate their decision making. This greatly enhanced level of activity reflects the growing number who are taking responsibility for promoting the understanding and application of ethical standards and guidelines.

Stephanie Feeney has come forward again, this time partnered with Nancy Freeman, to coauthor this new resource based on their wealth of knowledge and breadth of experience in the area of professional ethics for early childhood education. The value of their important contribution will be enhanced to the degree that many more of us take responsibility for understanding and applying the Code in our own practice and enticing others to integrate the Code into their decisionmaking.

Hymes, J.L., Jr. 1983. Foreword to *Who am I in the lives of children?* by S. Feeney, D. Christensen, & E. Moravcik. Columbus, OH: Charles E. Merrill.

Katz, L.G. 1978. Ethical issues in working with young children. In *Ethical behavior in early childhood education*, by L.G. Katz & E.H. Ward, 1–16. Washington, DC: NAEYC.

Katz, L.G., & E.H. Ward. 1978. *Ethical behavior in early childhood education*. Washington, DC: NAEYC.

Ward, E.H. 1977. A code of ethics: The hallmark of a profession. In *Teaching practices: Reexamining assumptions*, ed. B. Spodek. Washington, DC: NAEYC.

—*Marilyn M. Smith*
NAEYC Executive Director, 1973–98

Preface

Early childhood educators need to be aware of the impact of their behavior and to act in the best interests of those they serve. This is critically important because while their actions can lead to positive outcomes for children and families, they can also harm them. Knowledge of ethics and the NAEYC Code of Ethical Conduct are essential parts of the knowledge base of every caring and competent early childhood educator.

The NAEYC Code of Ethical Conduct provides a common framework for helping educators understand their moral commitments. It helps them to know and act upon the core values and ideals that guide those who work in the early childhood field in their professional relationships with children, families, colleagues, and society. It also assists them in understanding their ethical responsibilities and provides guidance for addressing ethical dilemmas that arise in the workplace (an ethical dilemma is a predicament that involves conflicting responsibilities and requires a choice between two alternatives, each of which can be justified). The Code alone, however, cannot guarantee ethical practice. Ethics must be embedded in daily practice.

Ethics and the Early Childhood Educator is written for those who work with (or are learning to work with) young children and their families in early childhood settings. The book is designed to introduce the NAEYC Code of Ethical Conduct and describe how to use it. Specifically, it is intended to help the reader

- become aware of the core values and ideals that lie at the foundation of the early childhood field,

- appreciate early childhood educators' primary commitment to the welfare of children,

- understand the ethical responsibilities of early childhood educators,

- learn to use the NAEYC Code to formulate well-reasoned resolutions to ethical dilemmas, and

- become adept at talking about ethical issues and justifying positions.

The book contains

- the text of the NAEYC Code of Ethical Conduct and Statement of Commitment,

- an introduction to the study of morality and ethics,

- the history and rationale for the development of the NAEYC Code and its two supplements,

- strategies for identifying and addressing ethical dilemmas,

- specific chapters addressing each of the four sections of the Code, and

- approaches for promoting awareness and use of the Code.

We are pleased that this book is being revised to include the 2005 revision of the Code and its 2011 update. The organization of the updated Code and most of the items contained in it are the same as in previous versions. Some items have been edited to reflect new thinking and terminology that has changed over time. Significant changes made during the Code's 2005 revision include the addition of a new Core Value that indicates that we as a field have made a commitment to:

- Respect diversity in children, families, and colleagues.

Other significant changes made during the 2005 revision of the Code are the addition of a number of items relating to the assessment of children. These reflect changes in the field since the Code was first written. At that time there was little cause for concern about the ethics of assessment, since most programs used anecdotal observations of children and samples of their work to evaluate development and learning. The current movement for educational accountability has led to increased, and often inappropriate, use of standardized testing in programs for young children. The following items were added to the Code in 2005 to provide early childhood educators with some ethical guidance for responding to current pressures relating to child assessment: I-1.6, I-1.7, P-1.5, P-1.6, P-2.6, P-2.7, P-2.8, P-4.5, and P-4.11.

The 2005 revision also, for the first time, made a distinction between our individual responsibilities to our communities and society and our collective obligations to advocate for young children and their families.

In the 2011 update, language was adjusted in I-2.3, I-2.5, I-2.8, I-2.9, I-4.7, P-1.3, P-1.4, P-2.2, P-2.4, and P-2.6, to reflect best practices in the field regarding family engagement. The 2011 update to the Code does not make significant substantive changes, but it reaffirms our commitment to partner with families. Items have been edited to highlight the importance of two-way communication between teachers/caregivers and families and to stress the importance of ensuring cultural consistency between children's homes and early care and education programs. Items P-1.4, I-2.3, I-2.5, I 2.8, I-2.9, P-2.4, and P-2.6 illustrate this new emphasis. These changes are summarized in chart format in the Appendix.

Our many years of experience in the field and studying ethics as it applies to early childhood education has convinced us of the importance of early childhood practitioners' commitment to ethical behavior. We hope that reading this book will help you recognize the moral dimensions of your work, support your efforts to shoulder your professional responsibilities, and guide your efforts to do what is right for young children and their families. We will have been successful if, in the words of Sally Cartwright, this book becomes "thumbed, marked up, and well used." It is meant to be a resource that helps you answer the question "What should the ethical early childhood educator do?" with skill and confidence.

—Stephanie Feeney and Nancy K. Freeman

Code of Ethical Conduct and Statement of Commitment

Revised April 2005, Reaffirmed and Updated May 2011

A position statement of the National Association for the Education of Young Children

Endorsed by the Association for Childhood Education International
and Southern Early Childhood Association

Adopted by the National Association for Family Child Care

NAEYC recognizes that those who work with young children face many daily decisions that have moral and ethical implications. The **NAEYC Code of Ethical Conduct** offers guidelines for responsible behavior and sets forth a common basis for resolving the principal ethical dilemmas encountered in early childhood care and education. The **Statement of Commitment** is not part of the Code but is a personal acknowledgement of an individual's willingness to embrace the distinctive values and moral obligations of the field of early childhood care and education.

The primary focus of the Code is on daily practice with children and their families in programs for children from birth through 8 years of age, such as infant/toddler programs, preschool and prekindergarten programs, child care centers, hospital and child life settings, family child care homes, kindergartens, and primary classrooms. When the issues involve young children, then these provisions also apply to specialists who do not work directly with children, including program administrators, parent educators, early childhood adult educators, and officials with responsibility for program monitoring and licensing. (Note: See also the "Code of Ethical Conduct: Supplement for Early Childhood Adult Educators," online at http://www.naeyc. org/files/naeyc/file/positions/ethics04. pdf and the "Code of Ethical Conduct: Supplement for Early Childhood Program Administrators," online at http:// www.naeyc.org/files/naeyc/file/positions/ PSETH05_supp.pdf)

The 2005 Revision and the 2011 Reaffirmation and Updating of the Code of Ethical Conduct

NAEYC's Code of Ethical Conduct is reviewed for possible revisions every 5 years. When the Governing Board of NAEYC determines that a full revision of the Code is necessary, the Association's process for position statement development and revision begins. This process involves extensive input and review by NAEYC membership, other early childhood education specialists, and, when appropriate, individuals with expertise in the area addressed by the position statement. Such was the case for the 2005 revision, in which a new Core Value, nine new Ideals, and fourteen new Principles were added to the Code—focused primarily on respect for diversity and concerns regarding accountability and child assessments.

In 2011, the Governing Board reaffirmed the 2005 Code and updated this position statement to reflect consistency with the "Supplement for Early Childhood Program Administrators." Specifically, Section III-C (Ethical Responsibilities to Colleagues/Responsibilities to Employees) was deleted, as these Ideals and Principles are addressed in the Supplement. Other minor modifications were also made to ensure clarity and consistency. In addition, changes were made to Ideals and Principles that regard responsibilities to families to ensure alignment with current family engagement best practices in the field.

Core Values

Standards of ethical behavior in early childhood care and education are based on commitment to the following Core Values that are deeply rooted in the history of the field of early childhood care and education. We have made a commitment to

• Appreciate childhood as a unique and valuable stage of the human life cycle

• Base our work on knowledge of how children develop and learn

• Appreciate and support the bond between the child and family

• Recognize that children are best understood and supported in the context of family, culture*, community, and society

• Respect the dignity, worth, and uniqueness of each individual (child, family member, and colleague)

• Respect diversity in children, families, and colleagues

• Recognize that children and adults achieve their full potential in the context of relationships that are based on trust and respect

Conceptual framework

The Code sets forth a framework of professional responsibilities in four sections. Each section addresses an area of professional relationships: (1) with children, (2) with families, (3) among colleagues, and (4) with the community and society. Each section includes an introduction to the primary responsibilities of the early childhood practitioner in that context. The introduction is followed by a set of Ideals (I) that reflect exemplary professional practice and by a set of Principles (P) describing practices that are required, prohibited, or permitted.

The **Ideals** reflect the aspirations of practitioners. The **Principles** guide conduct and assist practitioners in resolving ethical dilemmas.** Both Ideals and Principles are intended to direct practitioners to those questions which, when responsibly answered, can pro-

---

* *Culture* includes ethnicity, racial identity, economic level, family structure, language, and religious and political beliefs, which profoundly influence each child's development and relationship to the world.

** There is not necessarily a corresponding Principle for each Ideal.

vide the basis for conscientious decision making. While the Code provides specific direction for addressing some ethical dilemmas, many others will require the practitioner to combine the guidance of the Code with professional judgment.

The Ideals and Principles in this Code present a shared framework of professional responsibility that affirms our commitment to the Core Values of our field. The Code publicly acknowledges the responsibilities that we in the field have assumed, and in so doing supports ethical behavior in our work. Practitioners who face situations with ethical dimensions are urged to seek guidance in the applicable parts of this Code and in the spirit that informs the whole.

Often "the right answer"—the best ethical course of action to take—is not obvious. There may be no readily apparent, positive way to handle a situation. When one important value contradicts another, we face an ethical dilemma. When we face a dilemma, it is our professional responsibility to consult the Code and all relevant parties to find the most ethical resolution.

Section I:
Ethical responsibilities to children

Childhood is a unique and valuable stage in the human life cycle. Our paramount responsibility is to provide care and education in settings that are safe, healthy, nurturing, and responsive for each child. We are committed to supporting children's development and learning; respecting individual differences; and helping children learn to live, play, and work cooperatively.

We are also committed to promoting children's self-awareness, competence, self-worth, resiliency, and physical well-being.

Ideals

I-1.1—To be familiar with the knowledge base of early childhood care and education and to stay informed through continuing education and training.

I-1.2—To base program practices upon current knowledge and research in the field of early childhood education, child development, and related disciplines, as well as on particular knowledge of each child.

I-1.3—To recognize and respect the unique qualities, abilities, and potential of each child.

I-1.4—To appreciate the vulnerability of children and their dependence on adults.

I-1.5—To create and maintain safe and healthy settings that foster children's social, emotional, cognitive, and physical development and that respect their dignity and their contributions.

I-1.6—To use assessment instruments and strategies that are appropriate for the children to be assessed, that are used only for the purposes for which they were designed, and that have the potential to benefit children.

I-1.7—To use assessment information to understand and support children's development and learning, to support instruction, and to identify children who may need additional services.

I-1.8—To support the right of each child to play and learn in an inclusive environment that meets the needs of children with and without disabilities.

I-1.9—To advocate for and ensure that all children, including those with special needs, have access to the support services needed to be successful.

I-1.10—To ensure that each child's culture, language, ethnicity, and family structure are recognized and valued in the program.

I-1.11—To provide all children with experiences in a language that they know, as well as support children in maintaining the use of their home language and in learning English.

I-1.12—To work with families to provide a safe and smooth transition as children and families move from one program to the next.

Principles

P-1.1—**Above all, we shall not harm children. We shall not participate in practices that are emotionally damaging, physically harmful, disrespectful, degrading, dangerous, exploitative, or intimidating to children.** *This Principle has precedence over all others in this Code.*

P-1.2—We shall care for and educate children in positive emotional and social environments that are cognitively stimulating and that support each child's culture, language, ethnicity, and family structure.

P-1.3—We shall not participate in practices that discriminate against children by denying benefits, giving special advantages, or excluding them from programs or activities on the basis of their sex, race, national origin, immigration status, preferred home language, religious beliefs, medical condition, disability, or the marital status/family structure, sexual orientation, or religious beliefs or

other affiliations of their families. (Aspects of this Principle do not apply in programs that have a lawful mandate to provide services to a particular population of children.)

P-1.4—We shall use two-way communications to involve all those with relevant knowledge (including families and staff) in decisions concerning a child, as appropriate, ensuring confidentiality of sensitive information. (See also P-2.4.)

P-1.5—We shall use appropriate assessment systems, which include multiple sources of information, to provide information on children's learning and development.

P-1.6—We shall strive to ensure that decisions such as those related to enrollment, retention, or assignment to special education services, will be based on multiple sources of information and will never be based on a single assessment, such as a test score or a single observation.

P-1.7—We shall strive to build individual relationships with each child; make individualized adaptations in teaching strategies, learning environments, and curricula; and consult with the family so that each child benefits from the program. If after such efforts have been exhausted, the current placement does not meet a child's needs, or the child is seriously jeopardizing the ability of other children to benefit from the program, we shall collaborate with the child's family and appropriate specialists to determine the additional services needed and/or the placement option(s) most likely to ensure the child's success. (Aspects of this Principle may not apply in programs that have a lawful mandate to provide services to a particular population of children.)

P-1.8—We shall be familiar with the risk factors for and symptoms of child abuse and neglect, including physical, sexual, verbal, and emotional abuse and physical, emotional, educational, and medical neglect. We shall know and follow state laws and community procedures that protect children against abuse and neglect.

P-1.9—When we have reasonable cause to suspect child abuse or neglect, we shall report it to the appropriate community agency and follow up to ensure that appropriate action has been taken. When appropriate, parents or guardians will be informed that the referral will be or has been made.

P-1.10—When another person tells us of his or her suspicion that a child is being abused or neglected, we shall assist that person in taking appropriate action in order to protect the child.

P-1.11—When we become aware of a practice or situation that endangers the health, safety, or well-being of children, we have an ethical responsibility to protect children or inform parents and/or others who can.

Section II:
Ethical responsibilities to families

Families* are of primary importance in children's development. Because the family and the early childhood practitioner have a common interest in the child's well-being, we acknowledge a primary responsibility to bring about communication, cooperation, and collaboration between the home and early childhood program in ways that enhance the child's development.

Ideals

I-2.1—To be familiar with the knowledge base related to working effectively with families and to stay informed through continuing education and training.

I-2.2—To develop relationships of mutual trust and create partnerships with the families we serve.

I-2.3—To welcome all family members and encourage them to participate in the program, including involvement in shared decision making.

I-2.4—To listen to families, acknowledge and build upon their strengths and competencies, and learn from families as we support them in their task of nurturing children.

I-2.5—To respect the dignity and preferences of each family and to make an effort to learn about its structure, culture, language, customs, and beliefs to ensure a culturally consistent environment for all children and families.

I-2.6—To acknowledge families' childrearing values and their right to make decisions for their children.

I-2.7—To share information about each child's education and development with families and to help them understand and appreciate the current knowledge base of the early childhood profession.

I-2.8—To help family members enhance their understanding of their children, as staff are enhancing their understanding of each child through communications with families, and support family members in the continuing development of their skills as parents.

---

* The term *family* may include those adults, besides parents, with the responsibility of being involved in educating, nurturing, and advocating for the child.

I-2.9—To foster families' efforts to build support networks and, when needed, participate in building networks for families by providing them with opportunities to interact with program staff, other families, community resources, and professional services.

Principles

P-2.1—We shall not deny family members access to their child's classroom or program setting unless access is denied by court order or other legal restriction.

P-2.2—We shall inform families of program philosophy, policies, curriculum, assessment system, cultural practices, and personnel qualifications, and explain why we teach as we do—which should be in accordance with our ethical responsibilities to children (see Section I).

P-2.3—We shall inform families of and, when appropriate, involve them in policy decisions. (See also I-2.3.)

P-2.4—We shall ensure that the family is involved in significant decisions affecting their child. (See also P-1.4.)

P-2.5—We shall make every effort to communicate effectively with all families in a language that they understand. We shall use community resources for translation and interpretation when we do not have sufficient resources in our own programs.

P-2.6—As families share information with us about their children and families, we shall ensure that families' input is an important contribution to the planning and implementation of the program.

P-2.7—We shall inform families about the nature and purpose of the program's child assessments and how data about their child will be used.

P-2.8—We shall treat child assessment information confidentially and share this information only when there is a legitimate need for it.

P-2.9—We shall inform the family of injuries and incidents involving their child, of risks such as exposures to communicable diseases that might result in infection, and of occurrences that might result in emotional stress.

P-2.10—Families shall be fully informed of any proposed research projects involving their children and shall have the opportunity to give or withhold consent without penalty. We shall not permit or participate in research that could in any way hinder the education, development, or well-being of children.

P-2.11—We shall not engage in or support exploitation of families. We shall not use our relationship with a family for private advantage or personal gain, or enter into relationships with family members that might impair our effectiveness working with their children.

P-2.12—We shall develop written policies for the protection of confidentiality and the disclosure of children's records. These policy documents shall be made available to all program personnel and families. Disclosure of children's records beyond family members, program personnel, and consultants having an obligation of confidentiality shall require familial consent (except in cases of abuse or neglect).

P-2.13—We shall maintain confidentiality and shall respect the family's right to privacy, refraining from disclosure of confidential information and intrusion into family life. However, when we have reason to believe that a child's welfare is at risk, it is permissible to share confidential information with agencies, as well as with individuals who have legal responsibility for intervening in the child's interest.

P-2.14—In cases where family members are in conflict with one another, we shall work openly, sharing our observations of the child, to help all parties involved make informed decisions. We shall refrain from becoming an advocate for one party.

P-2.15—We shall be familiar with and appropriately refer families to community resources and professional support services. After a referral has been made, we shall follow up to ensure that services have been appropriately provided.

Section III:
Ethical responsibilities to colleagues

In a caring, cooperative workplace, human dignity is respected, professional satisfaction is promoted, and positive relationships are developed and sustained. Based upon our Core Values, our primary responsibility to colleagues is to establish and maintain settings and relationships that support productive work and meet professional needs. The same ideals that apply to children also apply as we interact with adults in the workplace.

(Note: Section III includes responsibilities to co-workers and to employers. See the "Code of Ethical Conduct: Supplement for Early Childhood Program Administrators" for responsibilities to personnel (*employees* in the original 2005 Code revision), online at http://www.naeyc. org/files/naeyc/file/positions/PSETH05_supp.pdf.)

A—Responsibilities to co-workers
Ideals

I-3A.1—To establish and maintain relationships of respect, trust, confidentiality, collaboration, and cooperation with co-workers.

I-3A.2—To share resources with co-workers, collaborating to ensure that the best possible early childhood care and education program is provided.

I-3A.3—To support co-workers in meeting their professional needs and in their professional development.

I-3A.4—To accord co-workers due recognition of professional achievement.

Principles

P-3A.1—We shall recognize the contributions of colleagues to our program and not participate in practices that diminish their reputations or impair their effectiveness in working with children and families.

P-3A.2—When we have concerns about the professional behavior of a co-worker, we shall first let that person know of our concern in a way that shows respect for personal dignity and for the diversity to be found among staff members, and then attempt to resolve the matter collegially and in a confidential manner.

P-3A.3—We shall exercise care in expressing views regarding the personal attributes or professional conduct of co-workers. Statements should be based on firsthand knowledge, not hearsay, and relevant to the interests of children and programs.

P-3A.4—We shall not participate in practices that discriminate against a co-worker because of sex, race, national origin, religious beliefs or other affiliations, age, marital status/family structure, disability, or sexual orientation.

B—Responsibilities to employers
Ideals

I-3B.1—To assist the program in providing the highest quality of service.

I-3B.2—To do nothing that diminishes the reputation of the program in which we work unless it is violating laws and regulations designed to protect children or is violating the provisions of this Code.

Principles

P-3B.1—We shall follow all program policies. When we do not agree with program policies, we shall attempt to effect change through constructive action within the organization.

P-3B.2—We shall speak or act on behalf of an organization only when authorized. We shall take care to acknowledge when we are speaking for the organization
and when we are expressing a personal judgment.

P-3B.3—We shall not violate laws or regulations designed to protect children and shall take appropriate action consistent with this Code when aware of such
violations.

P-3B.4—If we have concerns about a colleague's behavior, and children's well-being is not at risk, we may address the concern with that individual. If children are at risk or the situation does not improve after it has been brought to the colleague's attention, we shall report the colleague's unethical or incompetent behavior to an appropriate authority.

P-3B.5—When we have a concern about circumstances or conditions that impact the quality of care and education within the program, we shall inform the program's administration or, when necessary, other appropriate authorities.

Section IV:
Ethical responsibilities to community and society

Early childhood programs operate within the context of their immediate community made up of families and other institutions concerned with children's welfare. Our responsibilities to the community are to provide programs that meet the diverse needs of families, to cooperate with agencies and professions that share the responsibility for children, to assist families in gaining access to those agencies and allied professionals, and to assist in the development of community programs that are needed but not currently available.

As individuals, we acknowledge our responsibility to provide the best possible programs of care and education for children and to conduct ourselves with honesty and integrity. Because of our specialized expertise in early childhood development and education and because the larger society shares responsibility for the welfare and protection of young children, we acknowledge a collective obligation to advocate for the best interests of children within early childhood programs and in the larger community and to serve as a voice for young children everywhere.

The Ideals and Principles in this section are presented to distinguish between those that pertain to the work of the individual early childhood educator and those that more typically are engaged in collectively on behalf of the best interests of children—with the understanding that individual early childhood educators have a shared responsibility for addressing the Ideals and Principles that are identified as "collective."

Ideal *(Individual)*

1-4.1—To provide the community with high-quality early childhood care and education programs and services.

Ideals *(Collective)*

I-4.2—To promote cooperation among professionals and agencies and interdisciplinary collaboration among professions concerned with addressing issues in the health, education, and well-being of young children, their families, and their early childhood educators.

I-4.3—To work through education, research, and advocacy toward an environmentally safe world in which all children receive health care, food, and shelter; are nurtured; and live free from violence in their home and their communities.

I-4.4—To work through education, research, and advocacy toward a society in which all young children have access to high-quality early care and education programs.

I-4.5—To work to ensure that appropriate assessment systems, which include multiple sources of information, are used for purposes that benefit children.

I-4.6—To promote knowledge and understanding of young children and their needs. To work toward greater societal acknowledgment of children's rights and greater social acceptance of responsibility for the well-being of all children.

I-4.7—To support policies and laws that promote the well-being of children and families, and to work to change those that impair their well-being. To participate in developing policies and laws that are needed, and to cooperate with families and other individuals and groups in these efforts.

I-4.8—To further the professional development of the field of early childhood care and education and to strengthen its commitment to realizing its Core Values as reflected in this Code.

Principles *(Individual)*

P-4.1—We shall communicate openly and truthfully about the nature and extent of services that we provide.

P-4.2—We shall apply for, accept, and work in positions for which we are personally well-suited and professionally qualified. We shall not offer services that we do not have the competence, qualifications, or resources to provide.

P-4.3—We shall carefully check references and shall not hire or recommend for employment any person whose competence, qualifications, or character makes him or her unsuited for the position.

P-4.4—We shall be objective and accurate in reporting the knowledge upon which we base our program practices.

P-4.5—We shall be knowledgeable about the appropriate use of assessment strategies and instruments and interpret results accurately to families.

P-4.6—We shall be familiar with laws and regulations that serve to protect the children in our programs and be vigilant in ensuring that these laws and regulations are followed.

P-4.7—When we become aware of a practice or situation that endangers the health, safety, or well-being of children, we have an ethical responsibility to protect children or inform parents and/or others who can.

P-4.8—We shall not participate in practices that are in violation of laws and regulations that protect the children in our programs.

P-4.9—When we have evidence that an early childhood program is violating laws or regulations protecting children, we shall report the violation to appropriate authorities who can be expected to remedy the situation.

P-4.10—When a program violates or requires its employees to violate this Code, it is permissible, after fair assessment of the evidence, to disclose the identity of that program.

Principles *(Collective)*

P-4.11—When policies are enacted for purposes that do not benefit children, we have a collective responsibility to work to change these policies.

P-4.12—When we have evidence that an agency that provides services intended to ensure children's well-being is failing to meet its obligations, we acknowledge a collective ethical responsibility to report the problem to appropriate authorities or to the public. We shall be vigilant in our follow-up until the situation is resolved.

P-4.13—When a child protection agency fails to provide adequate protection for abused or neglected children, we acknowledge a collective ethical responsibility to work toward the improvement of these services.

Statement of Commitment*

As an individual who works with young children, I commit myself to furthering the values of early childhood education as they are reflected in the ideals and principles of the NAEYC Code of Ethical Conduct. To the best of my ability I will

- Never harm children.

- Ensure that programs for young children are based on current knowledge and research of child development and early childhood education.

- Respect and support families in their task of nurturing children.

- Respect colleagues in early childhood care and education and support them in maintaining the NAEYC Code of Ethical Conduct.

- Serve as an advocate for children, their families, and their teachers in community and society.

- Stay informed of and maintain high standards of professional conduct.

- Engage in an ongoing process of self-reflection, realizing that personal characteristics, biases, and beliefs have an impact on children and families.

- Be open to new ideas and be willing to learn from the suggestions of others.

- Continue to learn, grow, and contribute as a professional.

- Honor the ideals and principles of the NAEYC Code of Ethical Conduct.

---

* This Statement of Commitment is not part of the Code but is a personal acknowledgement of the individual's willingness to embrace the distinctive values and moral obligations of the field of early childhood care and education. It is recognition of the moral obligations that lead to an individual becoming part of the profession.

History of the NAEYC Code of Ethical Conduct and Statement of Commitment

This Code of Ethical Conduct and Statement of Commitment, April 2005 revision, was developed by the National Association for the Education of Young Children (NAEYC) with support from an advisory workgroup appointed by NAEYC's Governing Board.

The first Code for the Association was prepared under the auspices of the Ethics Commission of NAEYC. Stephanie Feeney and Kenneth Kipnis prepared a "Draft Code of Ethics and Statement of Commitment" and, following a five-year process involving NAEYC membership, the Code of Ethical Conduct and Statement of Commitment was approved by the Governing Board in July 1989. Revisions to the Code were adopted in 1992 and 1997.

Financial assistance for developing the original Code was provided by NAEYC, the Wallace Alexander Gerbode Foundation, and the University of Hawaii.

The Code is reviewed for possible revisions every five years, and the revision process involves extensive input and review by NAEYC membership and other early childhood education and ethics specialists.

The Statement of Commitment accompanying the Code is a personal acknowledgement of an individual's willingness to embrace the distinctive values and moral obligations of the field of early childhood care and education. It is recognition of the moral obligations that lead to an individual becoming part of the profession.

Glossary of terms related to ethics

Code of Ethics. Defines the core values of the field and provides guidance for what professionals should do when they encounter conflicting obligations or responsibilities in their work.

Values. Qualities or principles that individuals believe to be desirable or worthwhile and that they prize for themselves, for others, and for the world in which they live.

Core Values. Commitments held by a profession that are consciously and knowingly embraced by its practitioners because they make a contribution to society. There is a difference between personal values and the core values of a profession.

Morality. Peoples' views of what is good, right, and proper; their beliefs about their obligations; and their ideas about how they should behave.

Ethics. The study of right and wrong, or duty and obligation, that involves critical reflection on morality and the ability to make choices between values and the examination of the moral dimensions of relationships.

Professional Ethics. The moral commitments of a profession that involve moral reflection that extends and enhances the personal morality practitioners bring to their work, that concern actions of right and wrong in the workplace, and that help individuals resolve moral dilemmas they encounter in their work.

Ethical Responsibilities. Behaviors that one must or must not engage in. Ethical responsibilities are clear-cut and are spelled out in the Code of Ethical Conduct (for example, early childhood educators should never share confidential information about a child or family with a person who has no legitimate need for knowing).

Ethical Dilemma. A moral conflict that involves determining appropriate conduct when an individual faces conflicting professional values and responsibilities.

Sources for glossary terms and definitions

Feeney, S., & N. Freeman. 2005. *Ethics and the early childhood educator: Using the NAEYC code.* Washington, DC: NAEYC.

Kidder, R.M. 1995. *How good people make tough choices: Resolving the dilemmas of ethical living.* New York: Fireside.

Kipnis, K. 1987. How to discuss professional ethics. *Young Children* 42 (4): 26–30.

An Introduction to
Morality **and Ethics**

A s an early childhood educator, your work is complex, intense, and intimate. You work closely with children, colleagues, and families. You are expected to meet children's basic needs and nurture their physical, social, emotional, and cognitive development.

If you have spent much time working with young children, you probably have encountered some, if not most, of these situations:

- The behavior of a child in your classroom is rough and unruly. He has hurt other children. The other children become fearful, and parents begin to complain.

- A mother asks you to not let her 4-year-old son nap at school. She worries because she goes to work early in the morning and needs him to be able to fall asleep at night so they will both be rested and on time the next day.

- Your coteacher[1] is sometimes so inattentive and preoccupied with personal business that you find yourself supervising the children alone much of the time.

- The teachers you work with often gossip about children and their families.

- The mother of a child in your 2-year-olds group demands angrily that you tell her the name of the child who bit her son.

---

[1]In this book, the term *teacher* generally refers to the adult responsible for the direct care and education of a group of children in any early childhood setting (including infant/toddler caregivers and family child care providers). The term *practitioner* also includes administrators. The inclusive term *early childhood educator* refers to individuals in these roles as well as college and university faculty and other teacher educators.

- It has been raining for days. The children are restless, and you are having a hard time helping them stay busy inside. A teacher from another class offers to loan you a new, full-length, animated superhero video.

- The director and other teachers in your program expect you to have 3- and 4-year-olds do tedious worksheets all morning instead of hands-on activities that you have learned are appropriate for young children.

- The families of the children in your class want you to teach academic skills to 4-year-olds using large-group, primarily lecture and drill methods, instead of providing the developmentally appropriate hands-on activities you have learned are best for young children.

- A child in your class with whose family you have a very good relationship has just come to school showing signs of physical abuse.

- Your school principal expects you to administer a standardized paper-and-pencil test that takes more than two hours to complete to your kindergarten class of children from a low-income community (many of whom do not speak English).

> Have you encountered problems like these? Where did you turn for help? What would you say to a friend or colleague who is facing one of these situations and asks for your advice?

Early childhood educators are problem solvers

If you are an experienced early childhood educator, you are likely to be skilled at solving problems. You probably have faced situations like these and may have dealt with them by relying on your common sense and best judgment. Perhaps you responded by considering what you believed would be good for a particular child or fair to the other children in your class, or what you had done in the past. When facing ethical issues it is natural for you to rely on personal morality, good judgment, and past experience to lead you in a productive direction.

The study of morality and ethics begins with recognizing that decision making is profoundly influenced by personal beliefs, values, and morality. Early childhood educators confront the reality that much of their daily work involves, in some fashion, potential conflict. For example, novice teachers quickly learn that parents' views and those of colleagues don't always square with their own. Sometimes differences are minor and easily settled; occasionally they are substantial. When the stakes are high and resolutions that are fair and acceptable to everyone are hard to find, these situations can be particularly troubling. Early childhood educators, who tend to see their role as teaching and nurturing young children and not mediating differences between adults, often find it helpful to draw on their training and look to leaders in the field for guidance in dealing with predicaments. Even with training and guidance from role models, there are still going to be difficult and troubling situations—that's when a code of ethics can help you make decisions that are based on your knowledge of your responsibilities to children, families, colleagues, and society.

> Have you ever found yourself and a colleague coming up with very different solutions to the same workplace problem? How did you decide what to do? Where did you turn for help? What did you learn from the experience?

Personal attributes, values, morality, and ethics

This chapter explores the interplay between personal morality on the one hand and professional ethics on the other. In it we make a distinction between the personal attributes, values, and morality that you bring to your work and professional ethics, which involves agreed-on standards of behavior that are designed to guide your workplace interactions with children, parents, colleagues, and the community.

Personal attributes

You bring who you are as a person to your work with young children and their families. The temperament you were born with and your life experiences formed a unique combination to create your personality. It influences the particular ways you think, feel, and act.

A number of researchers have explored the personal qualities of effective early childhood educators. In their 1985 article "Effective Teachers of Young Children," Stephanie Feeney and Robyn Chun reported that researchers had found the attributes of good teachers of young children included a positive outlook, energy, physical strength, a sense of humor, flexibility, self-understanding, emotional stability, emotional warmth, and sensitivity (Feeney & Chun 1985). In the article "What Makes Good Early Childhood Teachers?"(1999) Sally Cartwright stated that love for children, training and experience, and respect for and trust in each child are fundamental attributes for preschool teachers.

In the 2008 *Young Children* article "Twelve Characteristics of Effective Early Childhood Teachers," Laura Colker surveyed 43 early childhood educators to obtain their perceptions about the personal characteristics of effective early childhood teachers. Based on analysis of their responses, she identified 12 characteristics of effective teachers—passion, perseverance, risk taking, pragmatism, patience, flexibility, respect, creativity, authenticity, love of learning, high energy, and a sense of humor.

While all of the characteristics listed in these articles are desirable, there is consensus that essential characteristics include kindness, the ability to nurture, self-awareness, respect for others, and fairness.

Personal attributes are very important; however, they are not enough to guide professional practice. This is true because many work situations call for more than a kind and caring personality. Even the most dedicated practitioners sometimes encounter situations that call for a difficult decision or come into contact with a child, family, or colleague with whom they find it particularly difficult to work. Personality conflicts or misinterpreted intentions sometimes make productive relationships difficult and call for professional problem-solving strategies.

Personal values

Values are qualities that individuals believe to be intrinsically desirable or worthwhile and that they prize for themselves, for others, and for the world in which they live (e.g., truth, beauty, honesty, justice, respect for people and the environment). Your priorities, the goals you set for yourself and for the children in your care, reflect your values.

You have absorbed your values as if by osmosis during a complex process combining your family background, religion, and culture with your life experiences. Think about the countless ways that your values guide your personal and professional life decisions. They influence major and minor choices. The things you do each day, what you choose to read or watch, the foods you eat, the places you decide to live, the job you do, and the kind of play you engage in are all influenced by your values. If you spend some time reflecting, you will be able to identify your personal values and see how they affect your life and work.

Personal values are the foundation for professional values. They guide many of the decisions you make in your workplace. Do you emphasize collaboration or individual achievement? Do you think nurturing creativity is worthwhile? Is social development as important in your classroom as cognitive development? Do you think that it is more important for children to learn to respect authority or to question authority?

If you are not clear about your own personal values, it is difficult to think productively about what you are trying to accomplish in your daily work with children and families. Thinking about the values you wish to promote for yourself and the children in your care is one hallmark of a professional educator.

Working in an early care and education setting, you discover quickly that not everyone has the same values related to children's behavior or adults' interactions with children. For example, how do you respond to the cultural differences in the ways parents discipline their children? Do you think that there is a *right* way for them to guide children's behavior and for children to show respect for their elders?

> Identify some personal values that have led you to choose a career working with young children. Think of some things you do with children and families that reflect these values. Think about a teacher who has positively influenced your life. What personal values did that teacher exhibit?

Personal morality and ethics

Morality can be defined as peoples' views of what is good, right, or proper; their beliefs about their obligations; and ideas about how they should behave (Kidder 2003; Kipnis 1987). From an early age people also learn that moral issues are serious and "concern our duties and obligations to one another . . . and are usually characterized by certain kinds of . . . words such as *right, ought, just,* and *fair*" (Strike et al. 1988, 3).

The roots of personal morality can be found in the early childhood years. You can probably identify the standards of behavior that the adults you looked up to established in your home, place of worship, your neighborhood. Telling the truth, being fair, putting family first, respecting elders, and treating others with respect are some of the earliest lessons that many people learn from their families and early religious experiences.

Ethics is the study of right and wrong, duty and obligation. It involves critical reflection on morality. Ethics is sometimes referred to as the science of moral duty. Ethics involves the ability to make choices between values and the examination of the moral dimensions of relationships. You are engaged in ethical deliberation, for example, when you see someone drop a $100 bill and consider the advantages and disadvantages of returning it to her.

Both ethics and morality involve the human ability to make choices among values and to make decisions about right and wrong. Though these terms are sometimes used interchangeably, in this book we use the term *ethics* to refer to conscious deliberation regarding moral choices.

> What are some of your strongly held ideas about morality? Where or from whom do you think you acquired them? Reflect on the experiences in your life that led you to develop these views of morality.

Professional values and ethics

It is important to understand that, although they are important, personal values and morality alone cannot always serve as the guide to professional behavior. This is because each person's experience is different. Not everyone has adopted the same values or learned the same moral lessons. Even those who hold the same beliefs may not apply them in the same way in their work with children. These realities make it clear that individuals need more than just their personal values and morality to deal with the ethical issues they encounter in their work.

Personal attributes, values, and morals form a necessary foundation for an individual's professional practice. Nevertheless, they need to be complemented with professional values and standards of ethical behavior for members of a profession to be able to speak with one voice about their commitments.

Professional ethics concern the kinds of actions that are right and wrong in the workplace and are a public matter. Professional moral principles are not statements of taste or preference; they tell practitioners what they ought to do and what they ought not to do. The sections that follow in this chapter address the role of professions in society and how professional values and ethics support individuals in doing their best for those they serve.

What is a profession?

To understand the term *profession* and the professional standing of early childhood education, it is helpful to begin by thinking about the different roles that are occupied in a society. In modern societies, responsibility for different aspects of the community's welfare is assigned to experts who provide services that are essential to people's well-being. Those who provide these services are called professionals. A professional's work involves expertise that comes from specialized knowledge. Because of their training, professionals may be viewed as the only ones who know how to provide this service. In other words they do something that other people cannot do for themselves or for one another.

The ideal for a professional is a calling to selfless service to the community, as opposed to a career based on serving individual self-interest. Therefore a professional is above all else a responsible person who is committed to providing a needed service to individuals and making a contribution to society as a whole (Cooper 2003; Kultgen 1988; Moran 1996).

A basic definition of a *profession* is that it is an occupation that promotes a significant social value (e.g., medicine and nursing are meant to promote the value of wellness; law, the value of justice; structural engineers, the safety of roads and buildings; and teachers, the value of learning) and that requires specialized educational training in some branch of learning or science. The work done by professionals tends to be respected because of the important contribution it makes to society.

Sociologists and philosophers who study professions have described a number of criteria that can be used to determine if an occupation is a profession (Bassett 2005; Cooper 2003; Feeney 2012; Kultgen 1988; Moran 1996; Nash 1996). Following is a brief description of eight criteria for identifying professions that are frequently included in the scholarly literature:

1. A profession has a *specialized body of knowledge and expertise* that is based on theory and is applied according to the particular needs of each case.

2. A profession requires practitioners to participate in *prolonged training* based on principles that involve judgment for their application (not a precise set of behaviors that apply in all cases).

3. A profession has rigorous *requirements for entry* into training that are controlled by members of the profession. Training is delivered in accredited institutions. Graduation from an accredited program is necessary, but professionals may also need to take an examination in order to receive a license to practice.

4. Members of the profession have agreed-on *standards of practice*—recommended procedures for dealing with situations that are regularly encountered in the workplace. A professional must be aware of and be guided by the standards of practice, but the decision about how to act needs to be responsive to the specifics of a situation.

5. A profession has a *commitment to serving a significant social value*. It provides a service that is essential to society and has as its primary goal meeting the needs of others. Professions are dedicated to the public interest, altruistic and service-oriented rather than profit-oriented.

6. Based on its important function and the specialized knowledge and skill of its practitioners, a profession is recognized as *the only group in the society that can perform its specialized functions*.

7. Because others in the society do not have the technical knowledge required to oversee their work, professions are characterized by *autonomy*—self-governance that results in internal control over the quality of the services provided.

8. A profession has a *code of ethics* that assures members of the society that it will serve the public good. A code is a document that spells out the profession's moral obligations to society and its guidelines for moral behavior.

Early childhood educators have differing levels of education, and they work in diverse settings that include public schools, child development centers (large and small, nonprofit and for profit, and with different kinds of sponsorship), and family child care homes. Despite this diversity, the field of early childhood education is working to advance its occupational status.

Substantial progress has been made in recent years on other criteria such as specialized knowledge and expertise, training based on principles, and standards of practice. The criteria of rigorous requirements for entry into the field, extensive training, and autonomy still present serious challenges. Because early childhood educators serve the important social function of caring for the nation's youngest and most vulnerable citizens, it is significant that the field has a code of professional ethics that its practitioners strive to live by. And early childhood education excels in the area of altruism—unselfish dedication to providing a valuable service to society. We are making significant progress toward attaining the standards that define a profession.

Professional core values

The core values of a profession differ from personal values. They are not a matter of preference, but instead are statements expressing what professionals hold to be most important. These values grow from the history and traditions of a field and help to shape its aspirations and beliefs about desirable practice. These values provide the foundation for discussion of professional ethics and the development of the moral guidelines for professions.

Professionals who deal directly with human welfare have a special obligation to behave in ways that nurture and benefit those they serve. Values that are essential for professions that are based on human relationships are caring, compassion, empathy, respect for others, and trustworthiness.

> Brainstorm a list of values that you think all early childhood educators should hold. (If possible, do this activity with one or two colleagues or classmates.) Compare your list to the list of Core Values in the NAEYC Code of Ethical Conduct. Consider why these lists are similar to each other or different.

What are professional ethics?

Because of their significant contributions to society, professionals are expected to commit themselves to behaving ethically. Personal morality, the moral compass each individual brings from childhood, informs much of our ethical decision making (Nash 2002). But personal morality that is based on individual values doesn't provide the answers for all the difficult situations early childhood educators face in the workplace. It doesn't tell you what to do about the child who is so rough that he hurts other children; what to do when a mother asks that her 4-year-old not be allowed to nap, even if he needs the rest; or any of the other dilemmas described at the beginning of this chapter. These situations all have a moral dimension and challenge teachers to do the right thing or find a fair solution.

As early childhood educators grapple with finding solutions to problems, they are likely to discover that their personal morality doesn't give them all the direction they would like to have. They realize that they need additional guidance from the combined wisdom and expertise of the early childhood field. The guidance that is needed can be found in a code of professional ethics that articulates the field's moral commitments. A code of ethics is based on moral reflection that extends and enhances the personal morality that practitioners bring to their work. Statements of professional ethics help individuals know what constitutes acceptable moral behavior and assists them in resolving the ethical dilemmas that they encounter in their work.

Codes of professional ethics

A code of professional ethics is based on critical reflection about professional responsibility carried on collectively and systematically by the membership of a profession. A code is based on the profession's core values, its sense of mission and conceptions of appropriate practice. It spells out ethical responsibilities and offers guidelines for resolving dilemmas involving conflicting responsibilities in the workplaces.

Codes of ethics vary among professions. Some are general and aspirational, while others provide specific guidance to practitioners, addressing the particular dilemmas that occur in their daily work. The NAEYC Code of Ethical Conduct was designed to address many of the recurring dilemmas found in the education and care of young children. This rather comprehensive approach was taken because childhood educators are a diverse group who work in many different settings. What tends to unite them is their commitment to children.

Lilian Katz, in her pioneering work (coauthored with Evangeline Ward) on ethics in early childhood education, states, "Codes of ethics give us courage to act in terms of what we believe to be in the best interests of the client rather than in terms of what will make our clients like us" (1991, 3).

She describes the main features of codes of ethics as the group's beliefs about

- what is right rather than expedient,
- what is good rather than simply practical,
- what acts members must never engage in or condone, even if those acts would *work* or if members *could get away with* such acts, acts to which they must never be accomplices, bystanders, or contributors. (1991, 4)

What Does a Code of Ethics Provide for a Profession?

- A vision of what practitioners should be like and how they should behave
- A statement of commonalities shared by everyone in the profession regardless of the setting they work in or the training they have received
- An introduction to the moral commitments of the profession for those entering it
- Guidance in making choices that best serve the interests of those served
- A tool to help members of the profession articulate their core values
- Help in understanding responsibilities and prioritizing obligations in order to find wise resolutions to ethical dilemmas
- Support for a professional who takes a risky (but courageous) stand
- A justification for a difficult decision
- A resource for generating discussion
- Information to the broader community about the profession's beliefs and values and what constitutes acceptable professional behavior
- Assurance to members of the society that professional practitioners will behave in accordance with moral standards (Feeney 2012; Feeney & Kipnis 1985; Katz 1995; Stonehouse 1998)

Professional codes of ethics are grounded in moral philosophy—the systematic study of moral concepts and moral principles. Moral philosophy examines concepts like *right, wrong, good,* and *evil* in their moral contexts. In Chapter 3, Addressing Ethical Issues, we will explore some approaches to moral theory that can help early childhood educators to reflect on possible resolutions to the ethical dilemmas that they encounter in the workplace.

A profession's code of ethics differs in important ways from the policies, regulations, and legal obligations that govern the field. A code provides guidance for individuals, not regulation of programs or other work settings. Moreover, members of the profession create their code, while individuals who are not part of the field being regulated frequently write the policies, regulations, and licensing requirements that govern it.

Morality is closely related to law, but there are differences. Not every aspect of professional morality is likely to be addressed by laws, and some laws may be determined to be immoral. The law is enforced by penalties imposed for breaking rules, while morality is enforced by conscience. Moral principles are, therefore, justified by reason rather than external authority.

Although regulations and laws are important in governing a field and providing basic protections for clients, and may overlap with a code of ethics in some ways, the profession's code represents a higher standard (Stonehouse 1998). A code describes the aspirations of the profession and the obligations of individual practitioners. It tells professionals how they should approach their work, what they ought to do and not do. The code is the tool that guides individuals in the process of practicing professional ethics.

Fortunately, the field of early childhood education doesn't leave its practitioners on their own to puzzle out how to behave ethically. Clearly stated standards in the NAEYC Code of Ethical Conduct provide a shared common ground for those who strive to do the right thing for children and families. The Code of Ethical Conduct addresses responsibilities to children, families, colleagues, and community and society by expressing standards of conduct based on core values. These ethical guidelines help teachers to weigh and balance conflicting responsibilities and find answers to the question "What should the ethical early childhood educator do?"

The NAEYC Code
of Ethical Conduct

I n the 1970s and 1980s, a growing awareness of the ethical dimensions of working with young children prompted the National Association for the Education of Young Children (NAEYC) to assume the lead in the development of a Code of Ethical Conduct for early childhood educators. This chapter describes the rationale for the Code, and its history, development, and provisions for its regular review and revision. It also shows how the Code has, since its first publication in 1989, responded to changes in society and the field of early childhood education and expanded its influence.

Why is a code of ethics important?

NAEYC's first book on ethics was published more than three decades ago (Katz & Ward 1978). It described four aspects of working with young children that had ethical dimensions and pointed out the need for a code of ethics for early childhood educators. The expanded edition (Katz & Ward 1991) of that early work was revisited and updated again as part of Lilian Katz's book *Talks with Teachers of Young Children* (1995).

Despite the many changes in society and in our field during the past 30 years, ethics remains important for the reasons Katz first identified in that early work: "the (1) power and status of practitioners, (2) multiplicity of clients, (3) ambiguity of the database, and (4) role ambiguity" (1991, 4).

Power and status of practitioners

The most compelling reasons for early childhood educators to have a code of ethics are young children's vulnerability and lack of power. Adults who care for children are larger and stronger, and they control resources and privileges that children want and need. Lilian Katz explains:

> It is taken as a general principle that in a profession, the more powerless the client is vis-à-vis the practitioner, the more important the practitioner's ethics become. That is to say, the greater the power of the practitioner over the client, the greater the necessity for internalized restraints against abusing that power. (1995, 241)

Young children cannot defend themselves when teachers or caregivers are uncaring or abusive. Very young children are not able to communicate in words. Even when older children can describe a caregiver's harmful or neglectful behavior, that does not necessarily mean their parents will understand the impact of that mistreatment, will know that what occurred was inappropriate, or will be able to ensure that harm or neglect doesn't happen again.

Katz (1995) offers the example of a 5-year-old who reported to his mother when she picked him up from child care that he had been given only one slice of bread during the whole day because he had misbehaved. Reportedly his mother told him that he should behave himself in the future if he doesn't want to be hungry. Such an incident illustrates the power that child care providers have over the children in their care and the vulnerability of young children who cannot meet even their basic needs without adult help. It also shows that family members do not always have appropriate expectations for children's behavior.

The dynamics of power and prestige may also influence how early childhood educators are treated by others and how they behave when they face challenges that arise when working with young children. The status of teachers of young children is generally low. Parents who would never think of questioning or second-guessing their doctor or lawyer may not acknowledge the specialized expertise of their child's teacher and may therefore expect her to automatically comply with a request that is contrary to her informed opinion.

What's more, some teachers and caregivers have had minimal specialized training in early care and education. As a result they may lack professional competence and confidence, which increases the likelihood that they may be tempted to behave unprofessionally. Katz points out that such temptations can include "regimenting the children, treating them all alike, intimidating children into conformity to adult demands, rejecting unattractive children, or becoming deeply attached to a few children" (1995, 242).

Because young children are so vulnerable, having a code is particularly important. It helps early childhood educators to understand their ethical obligations, resist temptations, and handle ethical dilemmas wisely.

Multiplicity of clients

Another reason a code is so important for early childhood educators is that they serve a variety of clients—children, families, employing agencies, and the community. Balancing her responsibilities to various clients is the challenge a teacher faces, for example, when she is asked to eliminate a 4-year-old's nap because of his mother's work schedule. Most early childhood educators would agree that their primary responsibility and allegiance is to the child, but when a mother requests that her needs take priority, it can make it hard for a teacher to decide on the best course of action.

In situations involving multiple stakeholders, early childhood educators must think through the priorities they assign to each client group. An early childhood educator facing the dilemma described above is likely to assign the highest priority to her responsibility to the child in her care, but there could be circumstances that would result in making the needs of the child's mother her first priority. In fact, in most instances when early childhood educators encounter a situation that requires them to prioritize between children or families and their employing agency or the larger community, they would agree that their primary obligations were to the children and families they serve.

A code of ethics helps teachers clarify the position of each client group in the hierarchy of their responsibilities and provides guidelines for determining in each situation which of the groups has the greatest claim to practitioners' consideration.

Uncertainty of the knowledge base

In discussing the knowledge base of early childhood care and education, Lilian Katz (1991) noted that neither state and local regulations nor the generally accepted body of professional literature reliably led early childhood educators toward clearly defined best practices. At that time no widely agreed-upon standards or assessment procedures existed to guide the work of early childhood educators.

Katz observed that in early childhood, as in other fields also lacking generally accepted standards of practice, this void created two problems. First, without a clear statement of accepted practice, practitioners would likely be swayed by one fad, then another, following whims that quickly become the norm. Second, practitioners who work without research-based standards of practice lack a necessary foundation for speaking with a unified voice to describe what is best for their clients. For the early childhood education field, this meant that it was difficult, if not impossible, to articulate which teaching practices were or were not beneficial to young children.

We can now say that significant progress has been made in the development of accepted descriptions of best practice. NAEYC's position statement on developmentally appropriate practice (NAEYC 2009) and accompanying book (Copple & Bredekamp 2009) offer a framework of principles and guidelines describing "which practices are most effective in promoting young children's learning and development" (Copple & Bredekamp 2009, ix). These guidelines were first published in 1986 and have been revised regularly since. They have assisted programs in defining quality for more than 25 years. While developmentally appropriate practice offers guidance that is widely respected and followed, it does not, and is not intended to, establish a baseline for responsible practice or provide procedures for assessing practitioner effectiveness.

Standards and accompanying measures of program quality are now often used to assess early childhood programs. NAEYC's research-based Early Childhood Program Standards (2005), which are the foundation for NAEYC Accreditation of Programs for Young Children, were developed and evaluated by leading educators. They identify 10 critical areas that high-quality care and education programs must address.

In addition, many states now have early learning standards or guidelines describing what young children should know and be able to do, as well as Quality Rating and Improvement Systems (QRIS) or other sets of standards that identify criteria used to assess program quality.

While it is true that existing standards have a significant impact on teachers' day-to-day practice, the fact remains that there are still no clearly defined and nationally agreed-upon standards of practice that apply to all early education settings.

Role ambiguity

Those who work with young children wear many hats. In the course of an ordinary day, an early childhood educator may be called to take on the roles of parent, teacher, doctor, referee, coach, and cook. When a teacher assumes all these responsibilities and meets the most basic needs of infants, toddlers, and young children day in and day out, the potential for tension between parents and caregivers is understandable. Katz suggests that "Responsibility for the whole child may lead to uncertainty over role boundaries in, for example, cases of disagreement with parents over methods of discipline, toilet training, sex-role socialization, and so on" (Katz 1995, 244). This means that early childhood educators have to manage a difficult balancing act—meeting children's needs for guidance and appropriate limits while supporting and reinforcing families' cultural beliefs and goals for their children.

What's more, early childhood educators are expected to sustain productive relationships not only with children, but also with children's families, colleagues, employing agencies, and the larger society that has entrusted them to care for and educate its future citizens. Balancing these diverse roles and relationships in the context of intense and intimate day-to-day work with young children and their families is a unique part of an early childhood educator's work.

NAEYC's Code of Ethical Conduct can help teachers negotiate this maze successfully. The Code grounds their efforts by delineating principles and ideals that help shape professional relationships and responsibilities to children, families, and colleagues. Chapters 4, 5, 6, and 7 explore these dimensions of early childhood educators' professional relationships in more detail.

In summary, a number of characteristics that are unique to early childhood educators' work made apparent the critical need for a code of ethics. The pages that follow describe the development of the NAEYC Code.

> Do you think that these four aspects of working with young children provide a strong case for the need for a code of ethics for the early childhood field? What experiences have you had with each one that support your view? Are there other characteristics of the early childhood education field that suggest the need for a code of ethics?

History of the NAEYC Code

NAEYC began conversations about professional ethics in 1976. At that time its Governing Board passed a resolution calling for the development of a code of ethics, but a clear commitment to the process did not emerge immediately. There was concern that having a code was not appropriate for a membership organization, that is, one open to anyone who wishes to join (in contrast to a professional organization to which only those with certain credentials may join). Instead of a code, the Board decided to develop a statement of commitment to express important values and ideals of the early childhood field that were "applicable to a diverse membership and designed to improve the quality of life for all children" (NAEYC 1977). The *Statement of Commitment* was printed on the back of the Association's membership cards from 1977–1992. A similar statement of commitment was created to accompany the NAEYC Code.

The topic of professional ethics emerged again in 1978 when NAEYC published *Ethical Behavior in Early Childhood Education* by Lilian Katz and Evangeline Ward. The book documented the need for ethical guidance in early childhood education and included a draft code of ethics that was never adopted by NAEYC.

In the 1980s interest in ethics in early childhood education continued to grow. Several NAEYC Affiliate Groups drafted their own statements of ethical conduct, and members began to request leadership from the national organization in addressing professional ethics. In 1984 NAEYC's Board established an Ethics Panel (then called the Ethics Commission) under the leadership of Stephanie Feeney. That group's first task was to explore and clarify the early childhood profession's understanding of its ethical responsibilities.

Three interrelated commitments regarding the development of an ethical code emerged in conversations at that time. First was that a code should be widely known and used. For this to happen, NAEYC believed its members needed to recognize that the code expressed their deeply held beliefs and feel that that they owned it. The second commitment was that the process of developing a code should involve as many NAEYC members as possible. And the third was the importance of a continuing commitment to systematic reflection on the ethical dimensions of practice even after a code had been adopted and was in use.

The Code's development

The first step in the process of developing the NAEYC Code of Ethical Conduct was publication in *Young Children* of a survey developed by Stephanie Feeney and Kenneth Kipnis, philosopher and professional ethics consultant to NAEYC (Feeney & Kipnis 1985). Many NAEYC members responded to the survey describing dilemmas that they had experienced in their work. Each day's mail brought moving descriptions of ethical issues confronting early childhood educators. Kipnis commented as he read the responses, "These people are in ethical pain." Some of the more troubling submissions were descriptions of a school that used oppressive discipline, a family who wanted teachers to harshly punish their child, and a center director who would not report suspected child abuse.

The majority of survey respondents agreed that attention to ethical issues and the development of a code of ethics should be an immediate priority. This interest and support confirmed to NAEYC that the time had come to embark on the process of developing a code.

Next NAEYC conducted ethics workshops in various locations across the country. Participants generated a list of the core values they believed exemplified the field of early childhood education and analyzed cases (based on those submitted in the survey responses) that involved ethical dilemmas. In addressing the cases, each group answered the question, "What should the 'ethical early childhood educator' do when faced with this situation?"

In May of l987 some of the most difficult dilemmas posed by survey respondents and addressed in the workshops were presented in *Young Children* (Feeney l987). The summary article asked readers what they thought "the good early childhood educator" should do in each situation. Readers' responses served as the basis for three subsequent articles in *Young Children:* "The Working Mother" in November 1987, with commentary by Lilian Katz; "The Aggressive Child" in January 1988, with commentary by Bettye Caldwell; and "The Divorced Parents" in March 1988, with commentary by Sue Spayth Riley. For each article, Kenneth Kipnis wrote comments from a philosopher's perspective.

By 1987 members of the Ethics Commission believed they had enough information about NAEYC's members' ethical beliefs to develop a code. Stephanie Feeney and Kenneth Kipnis, in consultation with the Ethics Commission and other ethics experts, drafted the Code of Ethical Conduct and presented it for comment at NAEYC's Annual Conference in November 1988. Revisions were made based on the comments received. NAEYC's Governing Board approved the first version of the Code in July 1989 as an NAEYC position statement and published it in *Young Children* in November of that year.

Organization of the Code

The NAEYC Code of Ethical Conduct consists of a preamble, a list of core values, and sections addressing early childhood educators' ethical responsibilities to children, families, colleagues, and community and society. It is accompanied by a statement of commitment, which is not a part of the Code but a personal expression of resolve to uphold the values and responsibilities shared by all early childhood educators.

The *core values* included in the Code are deeply rooted in the history of early childhood education. They express central beliefs, a commitment to society, and a common purpose. Based on the literature of the early childhood field and the values expressed by participants in the ethics workshops conducted during the Code's development, these core values make it possible for early childhood educators to reach agreement on ethical issues by moving from personal values to professional values that apply to us all.

Each of the Code's four sections consists of a brief introduction, a list of *Ideals*, and a list of *Principles*. The Ideals point the individual in the direction of desirable and exemplary professional behavior. The Principles (sometimes referred to as rules of professional conduct) identify practices that are required, those that are permitted, and others that are prohibited. Principles are the basis for distinguishing acceptable and unacceptable professional behavior.

Provision for revision of the Code

According to the Policy and Procedures Manual of the NAEYC Governing Board, the executive director of the Association "schedules periodic review and revision of all position statements to ensure currency and accuracy." This process ensures that the Code is responsive to changes in the Association's membership, the moral climate of society, and new challenges faced by the profession. The first revisions to the Code were proposed by the Ethics Panel and approved by the NAEYC Board in 1992 and 1997. The next revisions were proposed by an advisory workgroup appointed by the NAEYC Governing Board and approved by the Board in 2005. The Board most recently reaffirmed and updated the Code in 2011, deleting sections related to ethical responsibilities to employees (which are now included in a Supplement for Program Administrators), addressing issues that had emerged in the early years of the twenty-first century, and incorporating language that reflects the field's current emphasis on partnerships with families.

The Code has expanded to address other groups

When the Association developed the Code, time and resources were limited, and NAEYC decided to focus on issues arising in direct work with young children and their families. The NAEYC Code now has two supplements that extend its usefulness to other early childhood professionals. In the 1990s, the National Association of Early Childhood Teacher Educators (NAECTE), the American Associate Degree Early Childhood Teacher Educators (ACCESS), and the Division of Early Childhood of the Council for Exceptional Children (DEC/CEC) involved their members in studying and developing guidelines to deal with ethical dilemmas encountered in teacher education and other professional development settings (Feeney 1995; Ungaretti et al. 1997). This work culminated in the development of the NAEYC Code of Ethical Conduct: Supplement for Early Childhood Adult Educators. The boards of NAEYC, NAECTE, and ACCESS approved this supplement in the spring of 2004.

A Supplement for Program Administrators was developed with input from practitioners and the assistance of an advisory workgroup appointed by the NAEYC Governing Board. It was approved by the NAEYC Board in 2006, and was reaffirmed and updated in 2011.

> How did you first learn about the NAEYC Code of Ethical Conduct? What was your initial reaction to it? How have you used it in your work? In what ways have you found it helpful?

Another indication of the Code's contribution to the education profession is its endorsement by the Association for Early Childhood Education International (ACEI) and the adoption of the Code and both Supplements by the National Association for Family Child Care (NAFCC).

The issue of Code enforcement

Because a profession regards its code of ethics as part of the contract between professionals and their clients, most codes provide a mechanism for identifying ethical breaches and disciplining those who violate their profession's ethical standards. At this time there is no provision for enforcement of the NAEYC Code. Addressing violations of the Code would be difficult since NAEYC is a professional association that is open to everyone, rather than an organization limited to professionals who have satisfied specific requirements for admission.

When the NAEYC Ethics Panel addressed the issue of enforcement in 1990, it decided that the profession would be best served by focusing its efforts on disseminating the Code as widely as possible and encouraging its use by the membership rather than struggling with the issue of enforcement.

But even a code that is not formally enforced can provide significant benefits to a professional group. Margaret Coady observes,

> A code of ethics, particularly one which is publicized by representatives of the occupational group and is frequently discussed and elaborated, can have the function of helping define the responsibilities of particular occupational roles. . . . The existence of a publicly declared code can provide a focus for judgment and the sort of consultation and discussion which can assist and clarify it. (1991, 19–20)

In a letter to the Ethics Panel, NAEYC member Sally Cartwright eloquently expressed a vision of how the Code could be used:

> This Code, with honesty, heart, humor, and wisdom, is a strong affirmation of one's best professional course through the occasional vicissitudes of adult bias, twisted values, and painful decision. I, for one, want it right at hand, thumbed, marked up, well used. I need its support . . . the Code should function as an advisor and a guide.

The NAEYC Code of Ethical Conduct, even without enforcement, is a valuable resource for early childhood educators. The Code provides a unifying force in a field that is characterized by diversity—in the backgrounds of its practitioners, the training required of them, and the settings in which they work. Because of this wide diversity, the Code addresses issues quite specifically. It lays out the aspirations of the early childhood field, makes it clear what professional behaviors are required and prohibited, and offers guidance in addressing some of the ethical dilemmas that frequently occur.

The NAEYC Code makes explicit the standards of behavior that, when they become part of every practitioner's repertoire, will protect the children and families with whom they work and will lead to greater respect for those who work with young children.

> What would be the advantages of enforcing the NAEYC Code? What are the advantages of having it be voluntary? Which do you think is preferable and why? Do you think it is desirable to require everyone who works with young children to demonstrate knowledge of the Code and skill in applying it?

Addressing Ethical Issues

3

As you work with young children in child care programs, Head Start centers, schools, and family child care homes, you are very likely to find yourself dealing with situations that involve questions of morality and ethics. These situations may require you to weigh competing obligations to children, families, colleagues, community, and society or to make difficult, and sometimes unpopular, decisions.

This chapter is intended to help you develop skill in recognizing the ethical issues you encounter in your daily work, thinking about them, and working to find acceptable resolutions[1]. Discussions in the chapters sometimes focus on the responsibilities to specific children in an early childhood program; at other times they address educators' roles as advocates for children in their community, state, or nation. In either case, early childhood educators have an obligation to know and use their Code of Ethical Conduct to help answer the question: "What should the ethical early childhood educator do?"

In this chapter and the four that follow, we explore some of the ethical challenges that you, an early childhood educator, might encounter and consider how the NAEYC Code of Ethical Conduct can help you answer this question.

The NAEYC Code maps the ethical dimensions of early childhood educators' work. It helps individuals identify their responsibilities and guides

---

[1]We use the term *resolution* to emphasize that ethical dilemmas can be addressed with one of several acceptable courses of action. If the first strategy does not resolve the dilemma, the next one you try might. This contrasts resolutions with *solutions*—a single course of action that is intended to solve the problem.

decision making when they encounter predicaments that involve ethics: considerations of right and wrong, rights and responsibilities, conflicting priorities, or human welfare. These issues may surface in interactions with children, parents, and colleagues (including administrators) and in programmatic decisions.

Ethical responsibilities

The NAEYC Code identifies a number of explicit ethical responsibilities for early childhood educators. Some are actions we must take, others that we must not. Principles in the Code spell out our responsibilities to

> not harm children [by] . . . not participat[ing] in practices that are emotionally damaging, physically harmful, disrespectful, degrading, dangerous, exploitative, or intimidating to children. (P-1.1)

> not participate in practices that discriminate against children by denying benefits, giving special advantages, or excluding them from programs or activities. (P-1.3)

> be familiar with the risk factors for and symptoms of child abuse and neglect. . . . We shall know and follow state laws and community procedures that protect children against abuse and neglect. (P-1.8)

> not deny family members access to their child's classroom or program setting. (P-2.1)

> ensure that the family is involved in significant decisions affecting their child. (P-2.4)

> maintain confidentiality and . . . respect the family's right to privacy. (P-2.13)

> not participate in practices that discriminate against a coworker because of sex, race, national origin, religious beliefs or other affiliations, age, marital status/ family structure, disability, or sexual orientation. (P-3A.4)

> be familiar with laws and regulations that serve to protect the children in our programs and be vigilant in ensuring that these laws and regulations are followed. (P-4.6) (NAEYC 2011)

Multiple roles and relationships are characteristics of work in early childhood education, which makes teachers and others working with young children unique among educators and social services providers. A commitment to children's welfare is at the heart of our field. It is beneficial for children for early childhood educators to work in close partnership with their families. Educators also need to work effectively with colleagues, and to engage with the community and the larger society.

Ethical responsibilities are required and spelled out in the Code. The Code makes it clear, for example, that early childhood educators should never harm children; share confidential information about a child or family with a person who has no legitimate need for it; discriminate against a coworker because of sex, race, national origin, religious beliefs or other affiliations, age, marital status/family structure, disability, or sexual orientation, and should always know and follow laws or regulations designed to protect children.

Accepting these responsibilities means that sometimes you must take an unpopular position. For example, you may find that you must politely but firmly refuse to answer a volunteer's question about a child's family situation. You may need to challenge a director who has assigned you to supervise a larger number of children than is permitted by your state's licensing regulations. Or you may find that you cannot in good conscience support curriculum decisions or assessment practices that are not based on current knowledge and descriptions of best practices in respected publications like *Developmentally Appropriate Practice.*

Situations calling for these kinds of decisions make you realize that the right thing to do is not always the easiest or the most popular. The ethical responsibilities identified in the Code exemplify the high road of ethical behavior. The early childhood educator who wants to conscientiously embrace her profession's core values and ethical precepts must know about and act on these responsibilities. One of the most important aspects of the Code is its affirmation of what is right.

> Consider a situation that tempted you to do what was easy or popular or what others thought was correct rather than what you believed was right. What did you do? Were you able to keep sight of your responsibilities to children, families, and colleagues? How would you describe your thinking about it to someone new to the field?

Addressing ethical issues

When you encounter an issue or problem in the workplace, it is helpful to approach it using a two-part process. The first involves determining the nature of the problem. When you are clear about what kind of issue you are facing, you can act accordingly. If the problem is, in fact, an ethical dilemma, you move to the second part of the process—analyzing the situation with the goal of reaching a defensible resolution, one that can be justified based on the values of the field and its moral principles.

Part I—Determine the nature of the problem

The first step you need to take when you encounter a workplace problem is to ask yourself if it involves concerns about right and wrong, rights and responsibilities, human welfare, or individuals' best interests. When you determine that this is the case, you know that you are dealing with an ethical issue.

The next step in addressing the situation is determining if it involves ethical responsibilities or if it is an ethical dilemma. Responsibilities are clear-cut—they are things you must or must not do. Early childhood educators are sometimes tempted to act contrary to the responsibilities spelled out in the NAEYC Code. You might choose a particular action because it is easy or will make people like you. For example, think about how you might react if, on a rainy afternoon, another teacher offered to loan you a full-length superhero video. This offer may be tempting: the video would occupy the children on an afternoon when they could not go outside. However, deciding whether to show the video is not an ethical dilemma. Showing the video would be a violation of your ethical responsibilities to be familiar with the knowledge base of early childhood education and to provide worthwhile experiences for children. An ethical early childhood educator should refuse the offer and get out tumbling mats or fingerpaints instead of the DVD player.

When you ascertain that a situation involves ethics and you don't think it involves a responsibility, it is likely to be an ethical dilemma. An *ethical dilemma* is a situation for which there is more than one possible solution, each of which can be justified in moral terms (it can be described as a situation that deals with two "rights"). A dilemma requires a person to choose between two actions, each of which has some benefits but also has some costs. In a dilemma the legitimate needs and interests of one individual or group must give way to those of another individual or group; hence the expression "on the horns of a dilemma," referring to the two-pronged nature of these situations.

Ethical dilemmas are different from other workplace problems in several ways. First, a dilemma requires a choice between two or more defensible alternatives. Second, a dilemma may involve conflict between the values of a field as expressed in its code of ethics. For example, in the nap situation (introduced in Chapter 1) the teacher's knowledge of what the child needs in order to foster healthy development is in conflict with the ideal of respecting the preferences of families and creating partnerships with them. Dilemmas are also different from other problems encountered in early childhood programs because they rarely have a simple solution. An ethical dilemma usually cannot be solved quickly or by simply applying rules and relying on facts. You won't find easy solutions for the dilemmas you face in your early childhood workplace in this or any other book. You can, however, learn to work through these difficult decisions more skillfully with guidance from the NAEYC Code. When you are certain that you have encountered an ethical dilemma, you can move to the second part of the process—analyzing the dilemma in an attempt to find a justifiable resolution.

Part II—Analyze the dilemma

When you have ascertained that your workplace problem is an ethical dilemma, you can use the systematic process we describe in this chapter to help you to think it through. Deciding on the right course of action is usually challenging because a dilemma puts the legitimate interests of one person or group in conflict with those of another person or group. For an early childhood educator, that could mean placing the needs of a child above those of his parent or protecting the rights of the group even if doing so limits the options of an individual child. Finding a resolution to an ethical dilemma requires balancing the interests, needs, and priorities of one person or a group of individuals against the interests, needs, and priorities of another while trying to maintain positive relationships with everyone involved.

Sometimes when you encounter an ethical dilemma, you have to respond almost immediately. For example, if you are faced with an angry parent demanding to know who bit her toddler, you won't have time to do a lot of thinking about the appropriate response. You will need to respond on the spot. That doesn't mean, however, that your actions need be any less intentional than they would be if you had time to process the problem. It will be easier to respond under pressure if you are familiar with the NAEYC Code of Ethical Conduct and have had enough experience using it to make the process feel like second nature.

While some situations involving ethics may demand an immediate response, more often you will have an opportunity to think about what you should do. If you are dealing with a difficult situation, it is often helpful to talk it through with a friend, colleague, group of colleagues, director, or college instructor.

The truth is that neither knowing ethics nor responding in an ethical fashion is instinctive. Resolving dilemmas is not easy; ethical decision making is a skill that must be learned. Philosopher Kenneth Kipnis observes,

> It is not easy to work one's way through dilemmas in professional ethics. The choices we face are painful, it is often unclear where help is to be found, and people disagree about what to do. Ethics, like mathematics, requires disciplined thought. But as with any practical way of approaching problems, it can be taught. There are useful definitions to be learned, ground rules for discussion, and strategies that can help us reach resolution. As with most skills—cooking, skiing, throwing a pot, and using a computer—ethics can be taught. (1987, 26)

Thus, helping you become adept at applying the Code is the purpose of this book. In the next few pages we will describe a process you can follow when you encounter an ethical dilemma. The four chapters that follow demonstrate how to apply this decision-making process to some of the recurring ethical dilemmas teachers and caregivers face in their work with young children, families, and colleagues.

Identify the conflicting responsibilities. The first step in exploring an ethical dilemma is to identify the conflicting responsibilities. This entails thinking about all of the people involved (we refer to them as stakeholders). What does each person or group need? What are your obligations to each one? Will resolving the problem mean having to choose a course of action that favors the interests of one individual or group over the interests of another? What values are in conflict? If it becomes clear that you need to make a choice between stakeholders, you are dealing with a true ethical dilemma. In order to make a morally justifiable decision, you need to weigh and balance your obligations to each one.

Let's return to the example of the mother who wants the teacher to keep her 4-year-old from napping at school. The mother's request requires a response, so the teacher must choose *some* course of action. Upon reflection, she is likely to recognize that more than one *right* resolution is possible. This is the case because the values guiding early childhood educators' work address the importance of meeting the child's needs *and* honoring the family's wishes.

On the one hand, the teacher might decide to prevent the child from taking a nap, because she knows how hard it is to get to work in the morning and perform well on the job without having had a good night's sleep. If asked why she chose that course of action, she might say she was guided by her respect for the mother's wishes and the value she places on supporting families in the task of childrearing.

On the other hand, the teacher might refuse to honor the mother's request and allow the child to nap with the other children. If asked to justify her decision, she might say that she knows most 4-year-olds need a nap after lunch, and she has observed that this child needs to have a rest to have a productive afternoon. Either decision has reasonable justifications and involves some benefits and some costs.

How could the teacher negotiate a resolution that meets the mother's needs and the child's? What principles will guide the teacher as she balances these responsibilities? Which interests should be given the greatest weight if a compromise can't be worked out?

It may help you to see the conflicting obligations clearly if you summarize the choice between alternatives. You could think about the nap case like this: "Should I do what I think is best for the child **or** should I honor the mother's request?"

Have you ever been in a situation in which you had to choose between two alternatives, both of which could be justified? What were the competing interests? How did you respond? How did you think through what was the right thing to do? Was there a resource you referred to that helped you make the decision?

Brainstorm possible resolutions. When you understand the conflicting responsibilities involved you can move to the next step, which is to brainstorm some possible responses to the situation. At this point you will want to generate ideas without analyzing them or rejecting any. Make a list of all of the possible responses to the situation that you can think of. Next consider the feasibility and fairness of each one. You will probably find that some are unreasonably harsh (telling the mother no without considering what you could do to accommodate her request), and some are morally indefensible (letting the child sleep but telling him that "he almost fell asleep" so his mother wouldn't know he had napped). Quite a few of the responses you brainstorm may be courses of action that would solve the problem without forcing you to make a difficult decision (we describe this approach in the next section), and some may seem reasonable but would entail a hard decision that would require you to give the needs of one stakeholder (the mother or the child) priority over those of the other. Brainstorming will enable you to eliminate solutions that are unacceptable and to identify some possible next steps.

Consider ethical finesse. When you are clear about the conflicting responsibilities and have brainstormed some possible responses to the situation, you can begin to think about whether you can solve the problem in a way that will meet the needs of everyone involved. Finding a resolution without having to pick winners and losers is almost always better than having to make a difficult choice. Problems encountered in early childhood education can often be resolved amicably.

We use the term *ethical finesse* to describe this process of finding a way to resolve a problem that is satisfactory to everyone involved (Kipnis 1987). It can involve both creative problem solving and negotiation. In the nap situation, the teacher could help the mother develop more effective bedtime routines for the child or she could try letting the child take only a short nap. She could have him go to another classroom where children rest but do not sleep in the afternoon. Or the mother and teacher could agree on some kind of compromise.

Ethical finesse is a useful tool that can help to alleviate many problems; it is the first approach you will try in most situations. But it does not always resolve the problem at hand. Kenneth Kipnis offers this important reminder:

> Ethical finesse lets us avoid having to give up something precious. There is nothing wrong with it, indeed it is helpful to have a checklist of maneuvers for slipping out of a dilemma. But professional ethics does not consist entirely of finesse. Sometimes hard choices must be made. And so eventually we may have to reach the tough ethical questions. (1987, 29)

Each of the ethical dilemmas presented in this book considers possible ways for an early childhood educator to reach mutually acceptable resolutions using ethical finesse. Although we recommend ways that finesse might be used for resolving the dilemmas we present, in each case we will discuss the choice that would have to be made if finesse were not feasible or successful.

Look for guidance in the NAEYC Code. When you realize that a dilemma cannot be handled with finesse, you need to find a morally defensible resolution and act on it. At this point it is time to turn to the NAEYC Code for guidance. Begin by identifying which, if any, of the Code's Core Values apply to the situation. Core Values are not present in every dilemma—but when they are they will remind you that important foundational beliefs of the field are involved and should be honored.

The next step, after you have considered the Core Values, is to review the Code's Ideals and Principles. These offer more specific guidance that is based on the Core Values. This step will help you to clarify your obligations. Review the Code carefully to find guidance for addressing your dilemma and prioritizing conflicting values and responsibilities.

It is important to review the entire Code because some situations are addressed in several sections. This process will help you to clarify your obligations and will guide your efforts to prioritize the conflicting values and responsibilities that make this situation an ethical dilemma. At this point it will be helpful to list all of the items that are related to the situation.

Next you will need to ask yourself if you have all of the information you need to resolve the problem. You may want to check the accuracy of your information or gather additional facts by talking with and observing children, and talking with families, staff members, or specialists who have expertise relevant to the situation. Depending on the situation, you also may want to review school or center policies and pertinent laws.

Some frequently occurring dilemmas are addressed specifically in the Code. In many other instances the Code does not offer specific guidance, and you must work to come up with the best possible alternative. What the Code will help you to do is clarify the values and responsibilities that are in conflict, and help you to prioritize them.

Finally, you will decide how the relevant items in the Code can best be prioritized, come up with one or two resolutions that you think are justifiable, and consider the consequences and benefits of each one.

Evaluate possible resolutions using ethical theory. In Chapter 1 we discussed the body of literature created over the years by moral philosophers and others who study morality and ethics. Their work provides a lens through which early childhood educators can assess possible resolutions to the dilemmas they face. Rushworth Kidder points out that "merely to analyze a dilemma . . . is not to resolve it. Resolution requires us to choose which side is the nearest right for the circumstances" (2003, 23).

This section briefly summarizes three traditions of moral philosophy and accompanying principles for resolving dilemmas. Each of these approaches offers a different way of viewing a situation (Kidder 2003; Strike & Soltis 2009).

The first tradition of moral philosophy is called *utilitarianism* (sometimes called *consequentialism)* and derives from the nineteenth-century writings of British philosophers Jeremy Bentham and John Stuart Mill. Philosophers from this school of thought maintain that the ultimate basis for any judgment about the rightness or wrongness of an action should be the consequences of the action. In other words, the best action is the one that benefits the most people. Utilitarianism has been criticized on the grounds that it is impossible to foresee the consequences of an action and that even if a large number of people benefit from an action, others may be hurt by it.

The principle that can be drawn from this philosophical tradition is "Do what is best for the greatest number of people" (Kidder 2003, 154). The question you can ask yourself in your ethical deliberations is, "Are more stakeholders helped by this choice than are hurt by it?"

A second tradition is based on the writings of Immanuel Kant, an eighteenth-century German philosopher. His focus was on individual conscience and the *rightness* of an action, not on its consequences. Philosophers from this school believe that people should act so that their actions could become a universal standard that everyone should follow. They believe that acting this way creates the greatest good because it promotes right intentions and actions that can be universally accepted. Critics suggest that demanding that everyone always follow the same philosophical principles would be impossibly strict and that generally accepted principles can be in conflict with each other.

The philosophical principle that can be derived from this approach is "Follow your highest sense of principle" (Kidder 2003, 154). You can ask yourself these questions: "Is this the way I think that all professionals in our field should act?" "Is this action the best one for the profession as a whole?"

The third philosophical approach lies in the doctrines of all of the major religions, and it is often associated with Christianity. This tradition advises individuals to evaluate their actions based on the extent to which they promote the interests of others and preserve the fabric of relationships. This approach is consistent with ideas about women's morality, described by Nel Noddings (1984) and Carol Gilligan (1993) and referred to as the *ethic of care*. Critics note that the drawback of this approach is that it doesn't give direct guidance to individuals trying to make ethical choices.

The Golden Rule, "Do unto others as you would have others do unto you," is familiar advice with roots in the philosophical tradition of caring. As you deliberate about this perspective you might ask yourself, "Is this the way I would want others to treat me?" "Is this solution respectful of people and relationships?"

Considering these three schools of thought can help early childhood educators think about the impact of proposed resolutions to dilemmas, but they provide no clear-cut formulas for ethical actions. It sometimes helps to clarify the validity of a proposed resolution by asking yourself, "Could I justify this choice to the community at large if a reporter on the evening news asked me to?"

Decide on a course of action. You have a number of resources to draw upon as you weigh and balance all of the aspects of a situation. You have the personal values and morality that you bring to your work; you have the Core Values and ethical guidance of your profession expressed in the Ideals and Principles of the NAEYC Code; you have wisdom that comes from the historical traditions of philosophy; you may have the insights of the colleagues with whom you have consulted; and you have your own ability to reason. In the end, as Lilian Katz points out, "[All] we have at a given moment, in a given situation, is our own best judgment" (1990, 3).

All of these resources will come together to help you choose an ethically defensible course of action. It takes courage to make a hard ethical decision and stick to it. Careful consideration of the alternatives in combination with guidance from the field and your own best judgment should lead you to a sound decision that you could justify by referring to the NAEYC Code.

Remember that while there may be a number of acceptable resolutions to real-life ethical dilemmas, there also are unacceptable resolutions. If that were not the case, there would be little point in studying ethics. We hope that using the process presented here will help you avoid indefensible resolutions that violate the trust of children, parents, colleagues, or the community, and that it will help you arrive at well-reasoned and ethically supportable resolutions to the ethical issues you encounter in your work.

Implement, revisit, and reflect. When you share your decision with those involved, it is important to create a climate in which all parties communicate openly and honestly and listen to each other with care and courtesy. After the decision has been implemented, you can look at the success of the outcome and reflect on the process to see what you have learned from it. Kidder points out the value of this final step in the process: "This sort of feedback loop builds expertise, helps adjust the moral compass, and provides new examples for moral discourse and discussion" (2003, 186).

As you work your way through a dilemma, you may find that it has implications for policy, either within your program or in your community. Sometimes you will realize that a situation could have been avoided or would have been much easier to resolve if there had been policies in place that addressed it in advance. If this is the case, you will probably want to meet with others in your workplace to explore ways to make program policies more effective.

At other times you will realize that policies are needed in your community to better protect the interests of children and their families. Because early childhood professionals have a responsibility to stand up and be heard in the public policy arena, you may want to become active in addressing an issue you care about in your community. We will explore policy implications in the cases that we address in the chapters that follow.

Some advice about difficult dilemmas. Using the decision-making process described on pages 34–35 will often lead to a satisfactory resolution of an ethical dilemma. When you encounter a particularly difficult situation, it helps to talk it over with someone whose opinion you respect. You need and deserve a reality check, and the best helper is someone who is able to offer a critique and is willing to tell you if they think your view is flawed. This person may affirm that your inclinations are correct or offer insights you may have overlooked. Don't ask for advice from a person who will simply agree with you; a rubber stamp for your own ideas will not help you gain ground in your efforts to find the best, most ethical resolution.

In the rare event that you encounter a problem that has a legal dimension, such as a difficult hiring decision, you may want to discuss it informally with a lawyer—perhaps a member of your program's board or someone known to you in the community. A lawyer's advice is useful as you try to sort out the legal aspects of the dilemma. The situation may eventually require you to seek legal counsel, however. In that case, the lawyer's recommendations become an official legal record and can be used to explain or justify your actions.

> Think about a time when you made a hard decision as you addressed an ethical dilemma. Who were the stakeholders, and what were your obligations to each? What resources did you use to help you resolve the dilemma? What was the outcome? Was it successful?

Addressing a Workplace Problem

Part I: Determine the Nature of the Problem

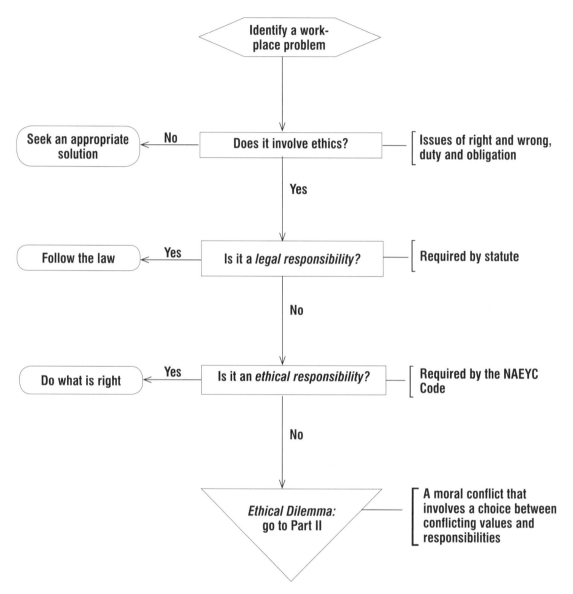

Part II: Analyze the Dilemma

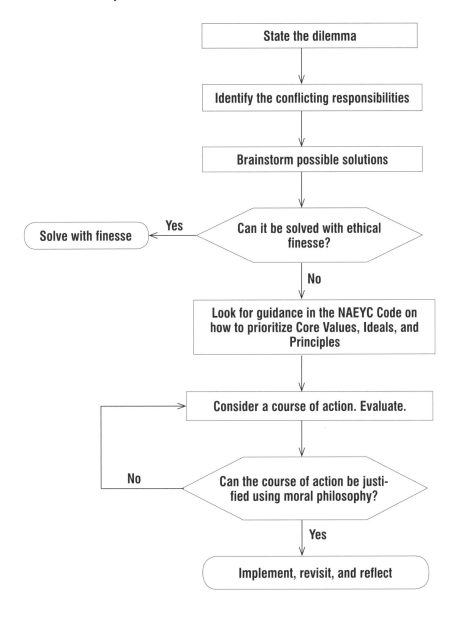

How ethical dilemmas are presented in this book

The next four chapters correspond to the four sections of the NAEYC Code. They address early childhood educators' responsibilities to children, families, colleagues, and community and society. Each chapter discusses ethical responsibilities relative to a particular section of the Code and investigates some recurring dilemmas. All of the scenarios described are based on real-life situations that have been shared with the authors over the years by teachers, caregivers, and administrators. The stories were adapted for use in this book and fictitious names added. We think you will find in them a ring of truth. Very likely you have worked with an Eric, a Niani, or a Mary Lou.

Each of the four parts of the Code addresses a different professional relationship. However, distinctions between these relationships are not that clear in real life. Ethical responsibilities in one area intersect and overlap with responsibilities to the others. Our obligations to children are related to our responsibilities to families. Our relationships with colleagues and the community relate to our responsibilities to children and their families.

We will analyze these cases in order to show you how the collective wisdom and expert guidance of experienced colleagues, expressed in the NAEYC Code, can assist you in resolving real-life dilemmas of your own workplace. The Core Values, Ideals, and Principles embraced by like-minded professionals can become guideposts in your work with young children and their families.

The scenarios described in this book are based in reality, but each situation is unique. The resolutions offered here are based on limited information available about a problem. When you face an ethical dilemma in your workplace, you will probably be dealing with a highly charged situation, and you will have much more information about it than we present on these pages. Compared with working through the situations described in this book, your task will be easier in some ways and more difficult in others. As you think about addressing an ethical dilemma, remember that usually there is not just one solution and that the resolutions offered here are not intended as "right" answers. They are meant to serve as models of a decision-making process you can use for finding sound resolutions to the real dilemmas that occur in your work.

4

Ethical Responsibilities to Children

Childhood is a unique and valuable stage in the human life cycle. Our paramount responsibility is to provide care and education in settings that are safe, healthy, nurturing, and responsive for each child. We are committed to supporting children's development and learning; respecting individual differences; and helping children learn to live, play, and work cooperatively. We are also committed to promoting children's self-awareness, competence, self-worth, resiliency, and physical well-being.

—NAEYC Code of Ethical Conduct and Statement of Commitment

NAEYC describes itself as "the world's largest association for those working with and on behalf of young children from birth through age 8" (NAEYC, n.d.a). Its mission is "to serve and act on behalf of the needs, rights, and well-being of all young children" (NAEYC, n.d.b). These NAEYC statements demonstrate why it is fitting that Section I of the NAEYC Code of Ethical Conduct addresses the early childhood educator's responsibilities to children, reminding all of us in the early childhood field that our first and most important responsibility is to children.

Those who care for and educate young children are in a unique ethical position because of the tremendous imbalance of power in their classrooms. While it is true that all teachers make decisions about how they will implement the curriculum, what instructional strategies they will use, and how they will manage the classroom, teachers of young children control many aspects of children's day-to-day lives. In addition to their teaching responsibilities, early childhood educators often establish daily routines related to toileting, eating, and sleeping.

Young children are not only dependent on their caregivers, they are also quite defenseless. The toddler whose diaper wasn't changed all morning because she ran behind the block shelf instead of coming to the changing table is not able to communicate that she has been neglected. A mother may not believe her 5-year-old when he tells her that he didn't get lunch because he didn't pick up his toys when the teacher told him to.

When we reflect on children's reliance on teachers, their special vulnerability, and their defenselessness, we are reminded of the importance of NAEYC's Code of Ethical Conduct. This statement of early childhood educators' responsibilities to children is critically important because the balance of power is tipped so heavily in the adult's favor.

Ideals

The 12 Ideals in the first section of the Code describe the aspirations of exemplary practitioners. They create a vision of the knowledge and skills early childhood educators should bring to their work, and the efforts they should make to ensure that the classroom they create respectfully nurtures all children's learning, growth, and development. These Ideals remind educators of their responsibility (1) to stay abreast of developing understandings of theory and practice in the early childhood field; (2) to appreciate children's vulnerability and each child's uniqueness, including culture, language, ethnicity, and family structure; (3) to ensure all children have access to programs that meet their particular needs while giving them opportunities to play and learn; (4) to use assessment strategies that support children's learning and development; and (5) to assist children and families as they move from one program to the next. The 2005 revision focused particularly on issues related to assessment, ensuring cultural consistency, and avoiding discriminatory practices. Five Ideals were added in that revision (I-1.6, I-1.7, I-1.10, I-1.11, I-1.12), and seven were revised (I-1.1, I-1.2, I-1.3, I-1.4, I-1.5, I-1.8, I-1.9). See the Code Comparison Chart showing revisions made in 2005 in the Appendix.

Principles

Eleven Principles (or rules of professional conduct) describe educators' responsibilities to children. They provide guidance and identify practices that are required, permitted, or prohibited. This section's very first Principle takes precedence over all others in the Code. It declares that "***Above all, we shall not harm children***." Other Principles in this section inform early childhood educators that they should create positive social and emotional environments that provide appropriate learning opportunities while supporting children's culture, home language, ethnicity, and family structure; implement inclusive enrollment practices; involve families in decisions that affect their children; use appropriate assessment systems that include multiple sources of information; make every effort to meet the needs of all children in their care; be vigilant for signs of child abuse or neglect, accept responsibility for reporting suspected maltreatment, and follow up on reported concerns; and take steps to protect young children from situations that could endanger their health, safety, or well-being.

The 2005 revision of this section of the Code's Principles revisits the themes addressed in the changes made to the Ideals at that time. They address assessment and the importance of achieving cultural consistency, and they strengthen the Code's prohibition on discriminatory practices. Two Principles were added at that time (P-1.5, P-1.6) and eight were modified (P-1.1, P-1.3, P-1.4, P-1.7, P-1.8, P-1.9, P-1.10, P-1.11).

The 2011 update revised two Principles (P-1.3, P-1.4) related to early childhood educators' responsibilities to avoid discriminatory practices, and to involve families in decisions that affect their children. See the Code Comparison Chart in the Appendix showing revisions made in 2005 and in 2011.

Typical ethical dilemmas involving children

Although early childhood educators' responsibilities to children are paramount, they create a relatively small percentage of the ethical dilemmas professionals face (Feeney & Sysko 1986; Freeman & Brown 1996; Rodd & Clyde 1991). Dilemmas in this category—concerning children only—are most apt to require early childhood educators to balance the needs of an individual child against the needs of the group or weigh the needs of a child with teachers' ability to meet these needs. These dilemmas challenge teachers to find solutions that take into account their responsibilities to *all* of the children in a group—children whose needs demand a great deal of attention, and those who tend to be overlooked or shortchanged as a result—and also to consider their responsibilities to themselves and to their colleagues.

The following pages describe two variations of this commonly reported dilemma. Our discussion applies the process described in Chapter 2 and identifies specific items in the Code to help early childhood educators think about what they should do when they face these kinds of dilemmas in their classrooms. Working through the process in these two cases will help you to think critically and systematically when you encounter similar situations in your workplace.

Case 1: The child with aggressive behavior

Eric is a large 4-year-old who attends a community-based child care program and sometimes engages in extremely aggressive behavior. When this happens, Eric frightens, or even hurts, other children. His teacher, Rose, has repeatedly discussed his behavior with the center director, who is sympathetic but has been unable to help. Eric's parents listen, but because they feel that his behavior is typical for boys his age, they won't seek counseling. A preschool specialist from the Department of Mental Health has observed the child, but none of her recommendations have helped. Eric's behavior can terrorize other children, and their parents are starting to complain to Rose. She is becoming stressed and tired, and her patience is wearing thin. Rose and her coteacher spend so much time dealing with Eric's behavior that they worry that the other children are not getting the attention they need and deserve.

> What is your first reaction to this case? To whom does Rose have obligations? What points should she take into consideration in making a decision? Brainstorm some ways that Rose might resolve this situation.

What should the ethical early childhood educator do?

Eric's story is a familiar one and a good beginning for our discussion of ethical dilemmas. Most early childhood educators have encountered an Eric! This case appeared in *Young Children* (Feeney et al. 1987) when articles about ethics were first published. It was analyzed in a later issue (Feeney et al. 1988) as part of the professional conversation surrounding the writing of the NAEYC Code of Ethical Conduct. The ideas presented here are adapted from reader responses to the case and from Bettye Caldwell's and Kenneth Kipnis's comments.

Determine the nature of the problem. Eric's teacher, Rose, faces an ethical issue because this situation involves her responsibilities to Eric and to his classmates. It forces her to consider how she will safeguard all children's rights to attend programs of early care and education that support their learning, growth, and development. It may also lead her to consider how to balance her obligations to Eric's family with her obligations to the families of all the children in the class, as well as to herself and other teachers who work with Eric.

As Rose examines her responsibilities to Eric and to the other children, she realizes she must consider several conflicting obligations. She believes in Eric's right to attend school with his peers and have a positive experience there. His behavior needs to be responded to appropriately, but he should be allowed to express his feelings and be considered an asset rather than a liability by his teachers and his classmates. Rose has a responsibility to be Eric's advocate and to help him become successful in school, but his behavior is stressful to her and is isolating him.

Rose also must carefully balance the needs of the entire class with Eric's right to participate in the program. She recognizes her responsibility to protect the other children in the group. They need to have a sense of safety and security and the opportunity to benefit from the program. Without an adult's help, Eric's classmates are unable to protect themselves from threats of danger and potentially harmful interactions with Eric.

Rose also has obligations to the families of the children in her care. Eric's family should have access to a program that can meet their son's needs. The families of the other children in the class are entitled to know that their children can have a positive experience and that they are not being threatened with injury.

This situation also raises important issues related to Eric's teachers' morale, ability to perform well, job satisfaction, and risk of burnout. We have learned that Rose is feeling stressed, tired, and her patience is wearing thin—her coteacher is probably experiencing similar feelings of exasperation and fatigue. If Eric's outbursts and aggressive behaviors continue, it is possible that one or both of them will resign in frustration rather than remain in a position where they find themselves unable to meet the needs of all the children. As Kenneth Kipnis points out, this alternative "is wasteful of the teacher's skill and dedication" (1988, 51) and one we should try to avoid.

Thus, Rose faces an ethical dilemma—meeting the needs of an individual child and his family is in conflict with meeting the needs of the rest of the children, their families, and their teachers. Each of these obligations is legitimate, yet if it is not possible to successfully honor them all, Rose may need to choose between opposing but defensible claims for her attention.

Consider ethical finesse. Fortunately, the situation involving Eric lends itself very well to ethical finesse (strategies for solving ethical dilemmas through skillful handling rather than having to choose between conflicting responsibilities). Before making any decision, Rose vows to try everything in her power to help Eric build the skills needed to function positively in the group. She identifies approaches that have been successful with other children and does some additional reading on child guidance. She pays special attention to being both gentle and firm with Eric.

Rose talks with Eric about how his outbursts affect the other children, and she encourages his classmates to express their feelings to him directly when he hurts or frightens them. While Eric is there, she gives attention and support to the child who has borne the brunt of his aggression. She tries pairing Eric with another child who can model appropriate prosocial behavior. She observes Eric's play carefully to learn to predict what triggers his aggressive behavior so that she can help prevent it or, when outbursts occur, to redirect Eric's energies before he frightens or injures a classmate. She reinforces Eric's positive interactions while coaching him in appropriate ways to express anger and frustration.

Rose also experiments with changes in the classroom learning environment, transitions, routines, and daily schedule to provide more structure for Eric. She modifies the curriculum to try making it a better match to Eric's abilities and interests. When none of these things seem to significantly improve his behavior, she works with her director to place him in another classroom for a week to see if a different setting, teachers, and group of children have a positive effect.

Rose arranges frequent conferences with Eric's parents to discuss his progress. She uses these opportunities to ask if his behavior at school is markedly different from his behavior at home and to determine if there are extraordinary stresses or medical conditions that could be causing his outbursts.

Rose doesn't expect every child to fit the same mold, but based on her professional knowledge and experience, it is clear to her that Eric's behavior is not typical of 4-year-old boys; she wants to help his parents see this. She has recommended to Eric's parents that they seek outside professional help, but they have refused. Because his parents do not agree that his behavior requires out-of-the-ordinary intervention, she provides them with information on child development and arranges for them to observe in her classroom and see for themselves how other 4-year-olds behave in a group setting. Rose hopes that these efforts will help Eric's parents realize that his present behavior is not typical. She wants to make them partners in her efforts to help Eric learn to deal more constructively with his feelings.

Rose's director arranges for a consultation with a specialist who helps Rose implement classroom-based interventions designed to modify Eric's behavior. These actions are all efforts at solving the problem without having to remove the child from the classroom or school.

Have you ever been in a situation when the needs of an individual child made it difficult to attend to the needs of the whole group? What did you do in that situation? What resources did you use to help you make a decision?

Look for guidance in the Code. Once it has become clear to Rose that the issues created by Eric's aggressive behavior are not going to be easily resolved using ethical finesse, she accepts the fact that she will need to take action to balance Eric's needs with those of his classmates. She knows it is important to turn to the NAEYC Code for guidance in resolving this ethical dilemma.

First she studies the Core Values and finds a number that apply to the situation she is facing:

- Appreciate childhood as a unique and valuable stage of the human life cycle
- Base our work on knowledge of how children develop and learn
- Respect the dignity, worth, and uniqueness of each individual (child, family member, and colleague)

Next, she turns to the Code's Ideals, paying particular attention to those related to Ethical Responsibilities to Children, but looking as well at those that describe her Ethical Responsibilities to Families. She notes the following Ideals that are relevant to the situation she is facing:

I-1.2—To base program practices upon current knowledge and research in the field of early childhood education, child development, and related disciplines, as well as on particular knowledge of each child.

I-1.3—To recognize and respect the unique qualities, abilities, and potential of each child.

I-1.4—To appreciate the vulnerability of children and their dependence on adults.

I-1.5—To create and maintain safe and healthy settings that foster children's social, emotional, cognitive, and physical development and that respect their dignity and their contributions.

I-1.8—To support the right of each child to play and learn in an inclusive environment that meets the needs of children with and without disabilities.

I-1.9—To advocate for and ensure that all children, including those with special needs, have access to the support services needed to be successful.

I-2.2—To develop relationships of mutual trust and create partnerships with the families we serve.

I-2.4—To listen to families, acknowledge and build upon their strengths and competencies, and learn from families as we support them in their task of nurturing children.

I-2.6—To acknowledge families' childrearing values and their right to make decisions for their children.

I-2.7—To share information about each child's education and development with families and to help them understand and appreciate the current knowledge base of the early childhood profession.

I-2.8—To help family members enhance their understanding of their children, as staff are enhancing their understanding of each child through communications with families, and support family members in the continuing development of their skills as parents.

She next identifies these relevant Principles in the section addressing Ethical Responsibilities to Children:

P-1.1—Above all, we shall not harm children. We shall not participate in practices that are emotionally damaging, physically harmful, disrespectful, degrading, dangerous, exploitative, or intimidating to children. *This principle has precedence over all others in this Code.*

P-1.2—We shall care for and educate children in positive emotional and social environments. . . .

P-1.3—We shall not participate in practices that discriminate against children by denying benefits, giving special advantages, or excluding them from programs or activities. . . .

P-1.4—We shall use two-way communications to involve all those with relevant knowledge (including families and staff) in decisions concerning a child, as appropriate, ensuring confidentiality of sensitive information.

P-1.7—We shall strive to build individual relationships with each child; make individualized adaptations in teaching strategies, learning environments, and curricula; and consult with the family so that each child benefits from the program. If after such efforts have been exhausted, the current placement does not meet a child's needs, or the child is seriously jeopardizing the ability of other children to benefit from the program, we shall collaborate with the child's family and appropriate specialists to determine the additional services needed and/or the placement option(s) most likely to ensure the child's success.

These items related to her Ethical Responsibilities to Families also prove helpful as she works to develop a plan of action:

P-2.4—We shall ensure that the family is involved in significant decisions affecting their child.

P-2.9—We shall inform the family of injuries and incidents involving their child . . . and of occurrences that might result in emotional stress.

P-2.15—We shall be familiar with and appropriately refer families to community resources and professional support services. After a referral has been made, we shall follow up to ensure that services have been appropriately provided.

Rose is confident that caring adults often can correct behavior problems when they are addressed promptly. She knows that teachers can help redirect most children's anger or frustration into acceptable expressions before they turn into out-of-control outbursts. However, Eric's aggressive behavior has persisted despite the extraordinary amount of time and energy that she and other staff members have devoted to helping him learn to control himself. Based on her professional knowledge and experience, she concludes at this point that Eric is so angry, strong, and uncontrollable that she cannot prevent him from hurting other children.

As Rose continues to study the Code for guidance, she realizes she has a professional responsibility to remind families that there are limits to the services her program can provide, an issue that is addressed in P-4.1, relating to her Ethical Responsibilities to Community and Society:

P-4.1—We shall communicate openly and truthfully about the nature and extent of services that we provide.

Rose is also becoming aware of the amount of effort she is putting into working with Eric. Not only is it diverting her attention from the other children, but she is becoming increasingly stressed and tired. She finds this additional item that is relevant to her situation. She does not have specialized training in working with children who have severe emotional needs.

P-4.2—We shall apply for, accept, and work in positions for which we are personally well-suited and professionally qualified. We shall not offer services that we do not have the competence, qualifications, or resources to provide.

Decide on a course of action. After trying several approaches to working successfully with Eric, carefully reflecting on her skills and expertise, and acknowledging that the other children's needs and the teachers' ability to perform well are suffering, Rose realizes she must prioritize the needs of the group. She decides that she must exclude Eric from her classroom until the family has taken appropriate remedial steps. As an alternative of last resort, this decision is supported by the Code, particularly P-1.7.

> Can you think of anything else that might have helped Eric learn to control his behavior in the classroom? Do you believe that the decision to insist that Eric's family find another setting for him was justified? What philosophical principles could Rose use to justify this decision?

Before taking the drastic step of excluding Eric, Rose meets again with her program director to share her careful documentation of Eric's behavior in the classroom, enlist the director's support, and discuss the best way to present the decision to the family. They schedule a meeting with Eric's parents to discuss the lack of improvement in his behavior and tell them that Eric may remain in the program only if the family seeks a counseling referral and if appropriate classroom assistance is provided for Eric. If the family is unwilling to pursue this course of action, the staff will help them find a more suitable program. Rose and the director hope that as a result of their efforts, Eric's parents will realize that his behavior is not typical for a 4-year-old boy and will agree to obtain help for him.

Eric's story demonstrates the difficult balance early childhood educators must achieve as they accept the responsibility of meeting the needs of all the children in their care. Teachers of young children sometimes need to acknowledge that they cannot be all things to all people.

The preceding case analysis is based on the assumption that Eric attends a private preschool program. These community settings are not likely to have access to special education services, and the teachers in them are unlikely to have specialized training in working with emotionally troubled children. If Eric were attending a public school, circumstances would be different. In that case, Rose's efforts would most likely revolve around making sure that Eric's parents understand and acknowledge his special needs and working within the system to secure an evaluation and the appropriate services that would help Eric to function positively in a classroom.

Implications for policy. Situations like this one involving Eric would be easier to manage if all programs serving young children—child development centers, large and small family child care homes, and primary classrooms—had clearly spelled-out and widely distributed policies regarding conditions under which children are referred for evaluation and when a child cannot be served.

Case 2: The child with emotional problems

Niani's play in Shana's classroom of 3-year-olds is limited to rolling a truck alongside the block area. During music time she howls, disrupting the activity whether or not Shana keeps her with the group. At naptime she bangs her head on the wall to put herself to sleep. Niani's parents have told her pediatrician about the concerns that school staff have expressed. He has assured them, to their relief, that "She will grow out of it." Shana and her assistant find that the class runs more smoothly, especially during group activities and naptime, if one teacher is always with Niani. Now another child's mother is upset, complaining that Niani disturbs her child and keeps Shana and her assistant from paying attention to all of the children.

> What is your first reaction to this dilemma? To whom does Shana have obligations? What points should she consider in making a decision? Discuss some actions she could take to resolve this situation.

What should the ethical early childhood educator do?

The dilemma posed by Niani's behavior is a variation of the one involving Eric. In both instances teachers are trying to balance their responsibilities to the group with those to an individual child. In both cases, the teachers grapple with their obligations to the families of all of the children in their classrooms, as well as the needs of staff who feel ill-prepared to meet this child's apparent special needs while working effectively with the entire group.

Determine the nature of the problem. Like Rose, Shana and her assistant face an ethical situation that requires them to balance their responsibilities to an individual child with their responsibilities to the group. They realize that they cannot do their best for the other children when Niani disturbs activities and requires almost constant one-on-one attention. They want to provide a quality program for Niani, and they also want to help her family recognize that her behavior is extreme and requires specialized intervention. In addition, they sympathize with the concerns expressed by the families of the other children in the class who feel that one child is taking too much of the teachers' time and energy.

Preschool is often the first place where families of children with special needs come into contact on a regular basis with children without special needs. Shana knows this and is sensitive to the fact that Niani's parents may have deep-seated fears about their child's development. Their doctor temporarily relieved them of their anxieties, so it's not easy or pleasant for them to accept Shana's recommendation that they get another opinion.

It is particularly difficult for an early childhood educator to disagree with the family's pediatrician. As Lilian Katz and Evangeline Ward (1991) observed, in most parents' opinion the doctor ranks higher on the ladder of professionalism than does their child's preschool teacher, and his or her advice is more likely to hold sway. But in this case it is important that Shana effectively communicate her concerns based on her specialized professional knowledge.

While recognizing similarities in these two cases, it is also useful to consider how they are different. In "Case 1: The child with aggressive behavior," Eric could be successful in school if he learned to channel his energy and control his aggression. Niani's behaviors, however, aren't those of a typically developing 3-year-old. Her teacher, Shana, knows that Niani's behaviors—playing exclusively with a single toy in a repetitive, ritualistic way; banging her head on the wall as a way to fall asleep; and howling during group music time—are all cause for concern.

Like Eric's teacher, Shana wants to create and maintain a safe and healthy setting that fosters all children's development. And, like Rose, Shana needs to seriously consider the effect that one child is having on the other children in her class.

Consider ethical finesse. Shana asks Niani's parents to observe in her classroom, for they may have had limited experience with children without special needs and could benefit from spending time with Niani's classmates. Shana believes that they will see how different Niani's behavior is from that of her peers. She hopes that as a result of this experience they will agree to seek expert advice.

If Niani's parents support a process that leads to a specialized plan for intervention, with Shana and her assistant as partners with appropriate therapists, then efforts to finesse this dilemma will have been successful. If Niani's parents follow through with this plan, her teachers can be hopeful that her needs will be met and that she and her classmates will be better able to benefit from their preschool experiences. They are well aware, however, that this child's behavior is extreme and that it is imperative that she receive services and assistance in the classroom if she is to continue in the program.

Look for guidance in the Code. The ethical imperatives guiding Shana's considerations of how to work with Niani and her family are like those that guided Rose as she worked with Eric. In this instance, however, Shana's concern that she does not have specialized training that prepares her to work successfully with children with special needs is paramount. She begins her analysis of this dilemma by referring to P-4.1 and P-4.2 (see above).

She finds additional guidance in the Core Values, Ideals, and Principles identified in the discussion of addressing Eric's out-of-the ordinary behavior. She appreciates each child's uniqueness and young children's vulnerability (see I-1.3 and I-1.4), but realizes that the current situation is diminishing the quality of the educational experience for all the children in her group and is not fostering their development (see I-1.5).

Niani's parents, like Eric's, want to believe these behaviors are nothing to worry about. Shana, her assistant, and the center director must be sensitive to maintaining their trusting relationship with Niani's parents (I-2.2). The reality is that Niani is not currently benefiting from this program, and the teaching team needs to face its responsibility "[t]o advocate for and ensure that all children, including those with special needs, have access to the support services needed to be successful" (I-1.9).

Shana has become increasingly aware that she and the rest of the school's personnel have a responsibility to do everything they can to ensure that Niani has access to appropriate interventions as soon as possible. Shana needs to collaborate with professional colleagues, as Rose did in Eric's case, to help the child's family access community resources for help in meeting their child's apparent special needs (P-2.15, I-4.2).

One Principle in the NAEYC Code calls for Shana's particularly careful consideration. It directs early childhood educators to make every effort to maximize the potential of the child to benefit from a program, but allows that "[i]f after such efforts have been exhausted, the current placement does not meet a child's needs, or the child is seriously jeopardizing the ability of other children to benefit from the program, we shall collaborate with the child's family and appropriate specialists to determine the additional services needed and/or the placement option(s) most likely to ensure the child's success" (P-1.7).

Decide on a course of action. At first Shana was determined to keep Niani in her classroom, but she has come to realize that she and her assistant lack the knowledge and specialized skills required to meet her needs while working effectively with all of the children in their class. Once Shana realizes that Niani needs specialized professional help that she is not qualified to give, she focuses her attention on providing Niani's family the information and assistance they need.

Shana and her director again meet with the family to discuss the situation. They offer to help arrange for Niani to be evaluated and to help the family access special services she apparently needs. They propose that if the family follows through, Niani may stay in the program until the evaluation is completed and arrangements have been made to implement needed interventions.

Shana, her assistant, and their director make it clear that, should the family not agree to an evaluation for Niani, their only other option would be to help the family find another placement. They hope, however, that this discussion will convince the family to seek appropriate help. They feel confident that once Niani has been properly evaluated, a treatment plan has been implemented, and specialized support services have been arranged, she can continue to participate in Shana's classroom. The only alternative they see to securing intervention services is helping the family find a more specialized setting.

> What is your reaction to the decision that Eric's and Niani's families must get help? What differences do you see between the two cases? Do you think that the decision was justified in each of the situations?

Case 3: Suspected child abuse (Child Abuse Situation I)

Trina, a 5-year-old in Dylan's class, shows the classic signs of potential abuse: multiple bruises, frequent black eyes, and psychological withdrawal. Her mother, who often seems nervous, gets angry easily, and is in a hurry at drop-off and pick-up, says that Trina falls often, but Dylan has not observed any clumsiness while Trina is at school. By law, teachers must report suspicions of abuse to their local child protective services agency.

What should the ethical early childhood educator do?

Child abuse is particularly difficult for most early childhood educators to acknowledge and handle calmly and competently. That is one reason situations involving suspected child abuse are some of the most frequently mentioned concerns identified by both teachers of young children (Feeney & Sysko 1986) and teacher educators (Freeman & Brown 1996).

Suspicions of child abuse require us to ensure children's safety, to understand the family's circumstances while we strive to develop and sustain positive relationships with them, and to access and rely on the resources available in our communities. This is the first of three cases addressing suspected child abuse that we will examine in this book. The topic will reappear in Chapter 5, which addresses our responsibilities to families, as well as Chapter 7, which considers our relationship with community institutions and responsibilities to community and society.

Open and honest staff discussions of ethical situations like the ones described in these three cases will help you sort through the issues, address strong feelings, and find the best resolutions to some of the most difficult decisions you will be called on to make in your career.

Our deliberations about suspected child abuse are always grounded in Principle 1.1 in the NAEYC Code:

P-1.1—Above all, we shall not harm children. We shall not participate in practices that are emotionally damaging, physically harmful, disrespectful, degrading, dangerous, exploitative, or intimidating to children. *This principle has precedence over all others in this Code.*

A dilemma describing suspected child abuse was first published in *Young Children* (Feeney 1987) and was addressed again in an article by the NAEYC Ethics Panel (1998). Ideas presented in the next paragraphs are drawn from reader responses to those articles, as well as numerous discussions of child abuse that we have had with early childhood educators over the years that we have worked on professional ethics.

> To whom does Dylan have obligations? What things should he take into consideration in making a decision?

Determine the nature of the problem. Dylan is facing an ethical and legal responsibility. If he has reason to fear that Trina is at risk of being harmed, he needs to recognize his responsibility to report what he has seen and heard.

Consider ethical finesse. At the point when Dylan noticed signs of possible maltreatment, he could have asked Trina's parents if their family was facing extraordinary stress, and he would have been wise to make an effort to learn if their expectations for Trina's behavior were reasonable. He also could have offered some suggestions about how to use positive guidance to help their 4-year-old learn how to behave if he were exhibiting behavioral problems at home. When symptoms of possible child abuse are clearly evident, however, it is not possible to make these kinds of efforts. Ethical finesse is appropriate only in cases less severe than Trina's. Now that Dylan has seen the bruises, black eyes, and evidence of psychological stress, he is facing a legal and an ethical responsibility—he has to act.

Look for guidance in the Code. The early childhood educator's responsibilities in this case are spelled out clearly in the Code.

These Ideals are related to our Responsibilities to Children and Families:

I-1.4—To appreciate the vulnerability of children and their dependence on adults.

I-2.2—To develop relationships of mutual trust and create partnerships with the families we serve.

I-2.6—To acknowledge families' childrearing values and their right to make decisions for their children.

Principles related to our Responsibilities to Children include

P-1.1—Above all, we shall not harm children. We shall not participate in practices that are emotionally damaging, physically harmful, disrespectful, degrading, dangerous, exploitative, or intimidating to children. *This principle has precedence over all others in this Code.*

Dylan may pause to consider whether he faces a conflict between the necessity of protecting the children in his care and his responsibilities to create respectful, trusting partnerships with families. Further examination of the Code, however, reveals two Principles that describe his responsibilities related to this suspected child abuse:

P-1.8—We shall be familiar with the risk factors for and symptoms of child abuse and neglect, including physical, sexual, verbal, and emotional abuse and physical, emotional, educational, and medical neglect. We shall know and follow state laws and community procedures that protect children against abuse and neglect.

P-1.9—When we have reasonable cause to suspect child abuse or neglect, we shall report it to the appropriate community agency and follow up to ensure that appropriate action has been taken. When appropriate, parents or guardians will be informed that the referral will be or has been made.

Dylan notes in particular that the second Principle requires not only that he file a report, but also requires him to follow up with his community's child protective services agency to verify that they have initiated an investigation.

Decide on a course of action. Dylan has been carefully documenting his observations of Trina's pattern of withdrawn behavior and the current signs of physical abuse. He discusses the situation with Charlene, the program director, who is well versed in the legal requirements and reporting procedures related to suspected child abuse. They both know that as a classroom teacher, Dylan is, by law, a mandated reporter. He must file a report with child protective services because he has reasonable cause (has seen visible signs) that leads him to suspect that abuse has occurred. He knows that it is not his responsibility to collect irrefutable evidence that Trina has been abused—that is the job of child protective services personnel. They will make the determination if Trina has been a victim of abuse and, if they conclude that intervention is appropriate, will take action to protect the child and provide family assistance. Reporting is mandated by law and is a responsibility explicitly stated in the NAEYC Code.

But the child care center's obligation doesn't end with making the report. Dylan and Charlene will check on the disposition of the case in the child protective services agency, continue providing nurturing support to the child as long as she is in the center, and work at keeping channels of communication open with the family. Both Dylan and Charlene want very much to maintain a positive relationship with Trina's family and would have liked to have had the opportunity to tell her mother that Dylan had noticed signs of physical injury and that the law required him to report it, but the situation has changed quickly. He knows that he must report his suspicion immediately. Dylan is aware that Trina is close to her maternal grandmother, and he has developed a trusting relationship with her as well, so he follows up the report by contacting her to talk about possible strategies to provide family support.

Early Childhood Programs Can Help Prevent Child Abuse and Neglect

Early childhood educators are often the first individuals outside of the home (besides the pediatrician) to interact with young children and their families. They can be a first line of defense against abuse and neglect. Consider these strategies that programs of early care and education can use to help prevent abuse and neglect.

- Build strong relationships with families before problems occur so that you have developed a foundation of mutual trust and respect when problems arise.

- Include statements in school handbooks informing families that teachers must watch for and report signs that indicate possible physical, sexual, verbal, and emotional abuse and neglect.

- Offer workshops and parenting classes to help family members learn positive ways of relating to and guiding their children to end patterns of abuse and neglect.

- Share publications and websites that offer information on preventing child abuse and neglect.

One group of early childhood educators responding to the 1987 article in *Young Children* wrote to the Ethics Commission:

> This case is much more clear-cut than many we are faced with. The situation will only get worse if it is not reported. We would not be able to live with ourselves if something should happen to the child while in the custody of the parents. We would rather err on the side of safety for the child.

A respondent to a *Young Children* scenario describing suspected abuse noted:

> In "real life" it's sometimes/usually very difficult to judge whether what you see and hear *should* make you suspicious, or whether you are overreacting out of a not-uncommon teacher tendency to protect a child from parents you simply disagree with, disapprove of, or dislike. (NAEYC Ethics Panel 1998)

Implications for policy. Having clear program policies that are shared with all families regarding the center's obligation to be alert to symptoms of child abuse and neglect and to report them can sometimes deter abusive behavior. At the very least, such practices inform parents of what they can expect if evidence of child abuse or neglect is observed. These policies should be in writing in the parent handbook and communicated when a family enrolls a child in the program. Some programs ask parents to sign a statement that they are aware that teachers are, by law, mandated to report suspected child abuse or neglect.

> What thoughts and feelings do you imagine Dylan and Charlene had when they realized they must report their suspicions of child abuse? Do you think every early childhood educator would act in the way they did?
>
> Identify some ways the NAEYC Code could be helpful in a situation such as this. Have you encountered suspected child abuse? What steps did you take?

Ethical Responsibilities to Families

Families are of primary importance in children's development. Because the family and the early childhood practitioner have a common interest in the child's well-being, we acknowledge a primary responsibility to bring about communication, cooperation, and collaboration between the home and early childhood program in ways that enhance the child's development.

—NAEYC Code of Ethical Conduct and Statement of Commitment

Early childhood educators work directly with children, but they always remain cognizant of the fact that every young child comes to an education and care setting as part of a family. All children have one or more adults who nurture and support them. The second section of the NAEYC Code of Ethical Conduct reminds us that while our primary responsibility is to the welfare and education of young children, we also have critically important responsibilities to the adults in children's lives. Recent NAEYC documents underscore the importance of cultural competence in the early childhood educator's obligations to families (NAEYC 2010). The 2011 reaffirmation and update of the NAEYC Code of Ethical Conduct highlights the importance of nurturing two-way communication between teachers and families and stresses the value of ensuring cultural consistency between children's homes and early childhood education programs.

Ideals

The Code includes nine Ideals relating to families. They lead early childhood educators toward a conscientious nurturing of relationships of mutual trust and the creation of bridges between families' cultures, values, and childrearing practices and our own. Educators also accept the responsibilities of seeking families' participation in decisions relating to their child, keeping them informed about how assessment data are being used, and building networks that give families opportunities to interact with other families and with professionals who support their parenting.

The 2005 revision of the NAEYC Code added two new Ideals (I-2.1, I-2.3) emphasizing the importance of basing our work with families on the field's knowledge base while welcoming and encouraging them to participate in the program. Revisions to existing items (I-2.3, I-2.4, I-2.5, I-2.6, I-2.7, I-2.8) stress the importance of recognizing families' knowledge and expertise, striving for cultural consistency, and effectively sharing our knowledge of young children's growth and development with families to enhance their parenting skills. Enhancing family engagement was the particular focus of the 2011 update of the Code. Four items in this section (I-2.3, I-2.5, I-2.8, I-2.9) were refined to strengthen the field's commitment to involving and communicating effectively with families, ensuring cultural continuity for children and families, and supporting families' efforts to build networks of support. See the Code Comparison Chart showing revisions made both in 2005 and in 2011 in the Appendix.

Principles

Fifteen Principles (or rules of professional conduct) relate to families. They include assuring families' access to their child's program and keeping them fully informed about relevant aspects of the program's operation. Ethical early childhood educators protect families from exploitation or breaches of confidentiality, remain impartial when there are familial disagreements, and stay prepared to make referrals to appropriate community resources when families need assistance in meeting their children's needs.

The 2005 revision added four new Principles to the NAEYC Code of Ethical Conduct (P-2.5, P-2.6, P-2.7, P-2.8). They call on early childhood educators to make every effort to communicate with families in a language they can understand, to use the information families share about their children to enhance program implementation, and to stress the importance of informing families about the assessments we do while ensuring the confidentiality of child assessment data. Revisions to seven other items (P-2.1, P-2.2, P-2.9, P-2.10, P-2.13, P-2.14, P-2.15) emphasize the importance of keeping families informed about the program and their children's experiences while in our care. They also include providing additional guidance related to information management and working with community resources that provide support services. The Code's 2011 emphasis on family engagement is reflected in modifications to three Principles (P-2.2, P-2.4, P-2.6). These changes stress the importance of informing families about the program's cultural practices and ensuring that families' contributions and involvement are considered. See the Code Comparison Chart showing Code revisions made both in 2005 and in 2011.

Typical ethical dilemmas involving families

An analysis of responses to a survey of NAEYC members conducted in the 1980s showed that ethical issues involving families were among the most prevalent. Early childhood educators reported many situations in which they felt torn between a parent's request and what they felt was best for the child. Other frequently encountered dilemmas involving families included handling suspected child abuse and neglect, dealing with divorce and custody issues, and making judgments about who needs access to sensitive information (Feeney & Sysko 1986). Since that survey was conducted, we have held many ethics workshops and classes and find that ethical issues involving families continue to be among the most frequently encountered and challenging situations faced by early childhood educators.

Because they occur so often, we have chosen to present two dilemmas that involve requests from a parent for a teacher to do something she does not think is in the child's best interests. In both cases the teacher has conflicting obligations to a child and to his or her family members. In this chapter we also present the second of three cases involving suspected child abuse. We hope that reading these cases will help you to think about how you could resolve similar situations that you might encounter in your workplace.

Complex-client situations

Generally professionals serve and have allegiance to one client. In a very few instances, a practitioner serves and has obligations to two clients. Notable among these are pediatricians and early childhood educators, who provide service to both the child and the child's adult family members. In these situations (which we refer to as *complex-client* cases), the professional has obligations to both the child and the family and may sometimes need to negotiate situations in which these obligations come into conflict.

A classic example of a complex-client situation occurs when a pediatrician interacts with family members who, for religious reasons, do not want a child to receive needed medical treatment. In early childhood education, complex-client issues generally involve requests from family members for an early childhood educator to do something that he does not believe is in the child's best interests. The dilemma involving a parent requesting that her son be kept from napping (discussed in Chapter 3 and again in this chapter) prompted Lilian Katz (Feeney et al. 1987, 18) to write about how early childhood educators can respond when parents ask that their child be excluded from usual classroom activities or routines. Katz notes that the mother's request is, in important ways, similar to other parental preferences that reflect lifestyle, religious, or other cultural values. There are similarities, for example, between the nap dilemma and that arising when a father asks that his son not be allowed to play with dolls or when a family doesn't want their child to participate in classroom birthday observances for religious reasons.

In cases such as these, Katz advises teachers and parents to listen to each other's opinions respectfully and to consider the child's probable reaction to being an exception to the rule. Will exclusion from a birthday observance make the child feel confused? Will being prohibited from playing with dolls inhibit a child's emotional development? When they can, teachers should make accommodations to honor parents' requests, provided no harm will come to their child or other children from doing so. Before a birthday party begins, for example, the teacher may invite the child to participate in an attractive alternative activity, perhaps in the classroom next door.

Above all, however, "when parental preferences require a child to be excepted from standard program procedures and the teacher judges the exception to jeopardize the child's well-being, the teacher must respectfully decline to honor the parents' wishes" (Feeney et al. 1987, 18). This decision is reflected in Principle 1.1 of the NAEYC Code of Ethical Conduct, which states emphatically that "we shall not harm children." This item takes precedence in all of our work with young children and their families. In the years that we have been working on professional ethics, early childhood educators have agreed that whenever the well-being of the child is in jeopardy that the child's needs must take precedence.

The early childhood field today has recommitted itself to partnerships with families, and the 2011 revisions to the Code of Ethical Conduct call for renewed efforts to ensure that families' views are taken into account and that there is respectful two-way communication between teachers and family members. The two complex-client cases that we discuss in this chapter will be considered in light of this new Code emphasis.

Case 4: The nap

Cathy, the mother of 4-year-old Timothy, has asked his teacher, Frances, to keep him from napping in the afternoon. She tells Frances, "Whenever Timothy naps he stays up until after 10:00 at night. I have to get up at 5:00 in the morning to go to work, and I am not getting enough sleep." Along with all the other children, Timothy takes a one-hour nap almost every day. His teacher says that he seems to need it to stay in good spirits through the afternoon.

> What is your first reaction to this situation? To whom does Frances have obligations? What factors should she consider in making a decision? Explore several avenues to resolving this situation.

What should the ethical early childhood educator do?

The nap case was one of six ethical dilemmas published in *Young Children* in 1987. Responses from readers and a commentary followed in a later issue of *Young Children* (Feeney et al. 1987). The discussion below is adapted in part from those sources. It has been a long time since this case was first addressed, but we find that the situation described in it continues to occur in early childhood programs and to be a concern for many early childhood educators.

Determine the nature of the problem. The nap situation involves ethics because it can be argued that it is right to honor the mother's wishes and that it is also right for a child to be allowed to get the sleep he needs. Frances feels strongly that the school must ensure that Timothy's physical needs are met. She is convinced that Timothy needs to nap. The dilemma lies in balancing Timothy's needs with his mother's needs as expressed in the request that he not nap in school. Although Timothy is her immediate concern, Frances is also committed to maintaining a good relationship with his family.

Timothy and his mother, Cathy, present a true ethical dilemma because their situation calls on Frances to weigh and balance conflicting values—meeting the needs of a child in her care and being responsive to the wishes of his mother. Cathy's request reflects priorities created by her work schedule, which she may not be able to control. Frances hopes to find a way to meet her professional commitment by sharing her early childhood expertise while honoring Cathy's needs and her desire to do what is best for her family as a whole.

Frances also considers the other children, posing questions to herself about the impact of possible decisions. What will Timothy do if he's not napping? Will his activities keep the other children awake? How will they react if everyone but Timothy is expected to nap?

The needs of Frances and the other teachers are also a legitimate consideration. Is naptime their only break in a busy classroom routine? Will the quality of teaching/caregiving be less if they do not have a chance for a change of pace? Will stress develop if teachers don't have a short respite from their responsibilities of managing a room full of busy 4-year-olds?

The first step in this process is for Frances to talk with Cathy about the request and listen carefully to her needs and concerns. In their meeting she will ask many questions so that she can fully understand the basis for the request and the family's situation. Once she is clear about the nature of the conflicting responsibilities to everyone involved, Frances begins to consider her alternatives.

Consider ethical finesse. Frances can immediately think of several things she could do using ethical finesse to resolve the nap issue without having to choose between the conflicting demands. Drawing on her professional knowledge, she discusses the value of naptime at preschool and asks about the family's bedtime routines. She asks Cathy if other family members, friends, or neighbors could play with Timothy while she prepares dinner so that he is ready for sleep as bedtime approaches. She suggests that chocolate and caffeinated soft drinks be eliminated in the evening, as these stimulants could be making it hard for Timothy to get to sleep. She recommends quiet activities, a bath, and a bedtime story to help Timothy settle down for the night. Frances hopes that in following these suggestions, Cathy can help Timothy be ready to go to sleep earlier and therefore eliminate the bedtime problem.

Frances also offers her support to Cathy, suggesting she will experiment with Timothy's nap routine at school. She tries variations of an earlier naptime, a shorter nap, and a long nap every other day. In addition to modifying the timing of Timothy's nap, Frances plans to try having him do quiet activities on his cot and spending naptime in another classroom where older children have quiet after-lunch activities but do not nap.

Look for guidance in the Code. Frances waits several weeks to give adequate time for her suggestions to Cathy and her own attempts to modify the naptime routine at school to improve the situation. She hopes these attempts can lead to a resolution to the dilemma that meets the needs of both mother and child. These attempts could very likely lead to a positive outcome, but in Timothy's situation nothing changes very much.

Frances is aware of the impact of her decision on Timothy's classmates and her teaching team's daily routine but knows she must focus her efforts on the responsibility to balance Timothy's needs with those of his mother. As soon as she realizes that she may need to choose between honoring the needs of the child or the wishes of the mother, Frances carefully reviews the NAEYC Code.

First she looks at the Core Values and finds a number of them are applicable to this situation:

- Base our work on knowledge of how children develop and learn
- Appreciate and support the bond between the child and family
- Recognize that children are best understood and supported in the context of family, culture, community, and society
- Respect the dignity, worth, and uniqueness of each individual (child, family member, and colleague)
- Recognize that children and adults achieve their full potential in the context of relationships that are based on trust and respect

The next thing Frances does is to turn to the Ideals in the sections of the Code that relate to Ethical Responsibilities to Children and Ethical Responsibilities to Families. She notes that the following Ideals have relevance to the nap situation:

I-1.4—To appreciate the vulnerability of children and their dependence on adults.

I-1.5—To create and maintain safe and healthy settings that foster children's social, emotional, cognitive, and physical development and that respect their dignity and their contributions.

I-2.4—To listen to families, acknowledge and build upon their strengths and competencies, and learn from families as we support them in their task of nurturing children.

I-2.6—To acknowledge families' childrearing values and their right to make decisions for their children.

I-2.8—To help family members enhance their understanding of their children, as staff are enhancing their understanding of each child through communications with families, and support family members in the continuing development of their skills as parents.

These Ideals confirm that she has important responsibilities to children's well-being and also to their families' needs and values. Frances wants to honor the family's wishes, but she is convinced that 4-year-old Timothy needs to sleep at least an hour each day if he is going to be able to function in the afternoon.

Next she considers the Code's Principles relating to children (those things that teachers must do or not do) with special attention to P-1.1, which takes precedence over all others in the Code.

P-1.1—Above all, we shall not harm children. We shall not participate in practices that are emotionally damaging, physically harmful, disrespectful, degrading, dangerous, exploitative, or intimidating to children.

She notes other relevant Principles:

P-2.2—We shall inform families of program philosophy, policies, curriculum, assessment system, cultural practices, and personnel qualifications, and explain why we teach as we do—which should be in accordance with our ethical responsibilities to children.

P-2.4—We shall ensure that the family is involved in significant decisions affecting their child.

Decide on a course of action. After her unsuccessful efforts to modify the nap routine, Frances is more convinced than ever that Timothy's emotional and physical well-being is dependent on his afternoon nap. Frances now faces a difficult predicament. Based on her review of the Code in combination with her best professional judgment, she decides she must give first consideration to the well-being of the child and will gently and respectfully tell Cathy that she cannot deprive Timothy of his nap.

When Frances meets with Cathy, she explains that after trying numerous alternatives she has concluded that being kept from sleeping would be harmful to Timothy and that he needs a nap to function in the classroom in the afternoon. Frances shares with Cathy the NAEYC Code and in particular the Principle that directs her not to participate in practices that are harmful to children. She tells Cathy that the collective wisdom of the early childhood profession must guide her in making this difficult decision.

Frances asks Cathy to respect her decision and urges that it not impair their positive working relationship. She reminds Cathy that children grow and mature quickly and that she will be alert to the signs that Timothy has outgrown his afternoon nap. For now, however, she says she must insist that the naptime routine remain unchanged.

There may be consequences to Frances's decision, and she realizes this. Cathy might decide to withdraw Timothy from the program and place him in another preschool that she believes will be more responsive to her needs. Depending on the supply and demand for child care in a particular community, the program director may put pressure on Frances to do whatever is necessary to honor Cathy's request. Teachers presented with this kind of ultimatum face the additional dilemma of standing alone in their decision rather than buckling to the demands of an administration with different priorities.

If you have ever stood in Frances's shoes, or can see yourself trying to resolve this dilemma, you appreciate the kind of backing the NAEYC Code provides. The Code adds the wisdom of a profession to a teacher's opinion. It may not make it any easier to make difficult decisions, but it offers support in knowing you are not alone when you stand firm in doing what you are convinced is right for the children in your care. We often say, "When your back is against the wall, the Code of Ethical Conduct can sometimes hold up the wall."

Policy implications. The nap situation might not have been so difficult if families had been informed when they enrolled their children in the program that naptime is a routine practice for 4-year-olds and that the center subscribes to the NAEYC Code of Ethical Conduct.

> What is your reaction to Frances's decision not to honor Cathy's request? Is this one of the ideas that emerged when you brainstormed solutions? What other resolutions did you think of, and how would you justify them? Have you been in a situation like this? How was the dilemma resolved? How did you justify your decision? What could Frances say to Cathy in this situation to communicate her respect and willingness to work collaboratively?

Case 5: Messy play

Ellie, the mother of Mia, a child in Alicia's class of 3-year-olds, has asked Alicia to keep her daughter clean and not allow her to participate in any art or sensory activities that are "messy" or "dirty." She tells Alicia that it is difficult to remove the dirt and stains that Mia brings home after doing art projects. She also says that it is important to her that Mia looks neat and clean when she comes to school and that messy play activities have led her to have to replace many of Mia's everyday pants, tops, and dresses. She also described the difficulty she has getting Mia clean at night when she has to meet her other family obligations.

> What is your first reaction to this situation? To whom does Alicia have obligations? What factors should she consider in making a decision? Explore several avenues open to resolving this situation.

What should the ethical early childhood educator do?

This second situation related to ethical obligations to families is also one that we have heard repeatedly from teachers. Like the nap case, this is a common occurrence in early childhood programs. It was described and analyzed in a course on professionalism and ethics taught at the University of Hawaii in

2010 and published in the Focus on Ethics column in *Young Children* (Feeney &
Freeman 2012). A number of NAEYC members, a college class, and participants
in two conference sessions on ethics weighed in on this case. Their input is
reflected in the discussion that follows.

   Determine the nature of the problem. The messy play situation is an
ethical dilemma because Alicia knows that it would be right to honor Ellie's
needs and wishes and also that it would be right to allow the child, Mia, to
engage in sensory and social experiences she enjoys and that contribute to her
healthy development. There is a conflict here between the needs of the child
and the needs of her mother. Alicia is faced with choosing between two "rights."
This is a complex-client case because it involves conflicting obligations to two
individuals to whom the early childhood educator has commitments.

   Alicia knows how much Mia enjoys participating in all the activities
provided during the school day—particularly the messy ones. And she firmly
believes that Mia needs these hands-on concrete activities to support her development and learning. Alicia also knows that it is important for Mia to have
opportunities to play with her classmates. She is a social child who enjoys the
give-and-take of the classroom and the choices she can make each day. Alicia
believes it would be a real disservice to Mia to limit her choices in the classroom, but at the same time she wants to honor Ellie's wish that Mia come to
school in clean clothes, and she certainly understands how hectic evenings
can be for working mothers.

   In this situation, Alicia has obligations to Mia, the 3-year-old who needs
hands-on learning; Mia's mother, Ellie, who has a busy work schedule and
deserves to have her wishes for her child respected; herself, a teacher who is
committed to meeting the needs of the children; and her colleagues, who have
an interest in the quality of the program and its relationship to its clients and
the community.

   The first thing that Alicia can do in this situation is to make sure that
she understands Ellie's request. She can arrange for a private talk with her in
which she seeks to understand the real reason for her request. It is important
at this point that she suspends judgment and listens attentively. A participant
in one of the workshops that discussed this case pointed out that true partnership involves seeking knowledge from others, including family members, not
just giving our own knowledge.

   Is the real issue that it is difficult to get Mia cleaned up for bed and for
school the next day? Or are there other reasons that have to do with the family's culture and values? Some families have a strong sense of pride in having
their child clean and well dressed at school, and they may worry that a dirty,
unkempt child will reinforce negative stereotypes of their ethnic or cultural
group rather than provide a positive example. Other families may feel that

sending a child to school well dressed and groomed indicates appropriate respect for the school as an institution.

The quality of the communication is of utmost importance in this situation. Alicia needs to engage in two-way dialogue and listen carefully without discounting the mother's wishes or judging her viewpoint. Revisions to the NAEYC Code underscore how critically important it is for teachers to understand the parent's views and to be aware of and respect any cultural differences. Once Alicia is sure that she really understands the meaning of Ellie's request, she can begin to think about whether ethical finesse can be applied in order to arrive at a "win-win" outcome.

Consider ethical finesse. Alicia can see that this situation lends itself very well to the use of ethical finesse and could very well end in a happy resolution. If Alicia determines that Ellie's request really is about how hard it is to get Mia cleaned up at night, then there are a number of things that she can do to help her while continuing to allow Mia to participate in messy activities. Ellie could send clean clothes from home and the staff could help Mia wash and change before she leaves school; Mia's clothing could be washed at school (if there were a washing machine); or Mia's hair could be tied back. The school could provide big shirts or smocks for all of the children to wear and even use hand-lotion type protection available online and in art stores for the children.

It would also be possible to use finesse in this situation by modifying some classroom activities. The school could provide materials that are easier to clean—washable paint, playdough instead of clay, washable markers, and other art media that do not stick to people or clothes. The program can set up water for painting on sidewalks or fences. Children could learn some ways to control the materials in order not to get so dirty. Teachers could modify the school program by scheduling messy activities early in the day or providing longer transitions between activities so there is more time for thorough cleanup. Or they could schedule a once-a-week "messy day" when it is convenient for Ellie.

It is likely that ethical finesse is all that is needed in this situation. But when we address ethical dilemmas, it is always a good idea to think about what would happen if finesse does not work.

Look for guidance in the Code. When finesse does not resolve the situation, Alicia turns to the NAEYC Code of Ethics for guidance. When she looks at the Core Values she finds that, as in the previous case, quite a few of them are applicable to this situation:

- Base our work on knowledge of how children develop and learn
- Appreciate and support the bond between the child and family
- Recognize that children are best understood and supported in the context of family, culture, community, and society

- Respect the dignity, worth, and uniqueness of each individual (child, family member, and colleague)
- Recognize that children and adults achieve their full potential in the context of relationships that are based on trust and respect

The number of Core Values that relate to the situation suggests that Alicia needs to do some serious thinking about how to prioritize them. The NAEYC Code emphasizes the early childhood education field's strong historical commitment to all areas of children's development and an equally strong commitment (highlighted in the Code's 2011 reaffirmation) to respect the needs and wishes of children's families and to work in close collaboration with them. In this situation Alicia is faced with the thorny dilemma of determining whether it is more important to honor the relationship with the mother or the needs of the child.

The first option, to let the child continue to participate in messy activities, could be supported by a number of items in the NAEYC Code. NAEYC has taken the position in its Code of Ethical Conduct that the child's well-being is of primary concern and that under no circumstances should a child be harmed. As in all ethical situations that involve children, Alicia must first consider P-1.1:

Above all, we shall not harm children. We shall not participate in practices that are emotionally damaging, physically harmful, disrespectful, degrading, dangerous, exploitative, or intimidating to children. *This principle has precedence over all others in this Code.*

Other ethical responsibilities to children reflected in Ideals in the Code support the decision to let Mia continue to participate in sensory and art activities:

I-1.2—To base program practices upon current knowledge and research in the field of early childhood education, child development, and related disciplines, as well as on particular knowledge of each child.

I-1.5—To create and maintain safe and healthy settings that foster children's social, emotional, cognitive, and physical development and that respect their dignity and their contributions.

If, after careful observation and reflection, Alicia determined that it would be detrimental to Mia not to be allowed to engage in messy activities, then she would be justified in declining this mother's request. She could argue that excluding Mia from sensory activities would deprive her of meaningful learning experiences and could be harmful if she had issues with sensory integration or emotionally damaging if she were deprived of significant peer interactions.

The second possible course of action, to do what Ellie asked and prevent Mia from participating in messy activities, can be justified by reference to Code items that highlight the importance of respect for and collaboration with families. These include

I-2.2—To develop relationships of mutual trust and create partnerships with the families we serve.

I-2.5—To respect the dignity and preferences of each family. . . .

I-2.6—To acknowledge families' childrearing values and their right to make decisions for their children.

P-2.6—As families share information with us about their children and families, we shall ensure that families' input is an important contribution to the planning and implementation of the program.

Decide on a course of action. If Alicia concludes that it would not be harmful to Mia to restrict her access to sensory materials, she would be justified in honoring Ellie's request. This decision would be supported if she felt that honoring parental wishes would communicate respect and increase the likelihood of a productive relationship in the future. Some early childhood leaders today make the case that respect for the parent and developing a bond between teacher and family is as important as meeting a child's immediate needs.

In order to show respect for the mother's wishes, Alicia could curtail messy play for a while or redirect Mia to other kinds of activities while she engaged in a dialogue and problem-solving process with Ellie. Such a process would involve acknowledging Ellie's feelings and asking for her suggestions about how to handle the situation. If Alicia limited Mia's access to activities, it would be important not to single her out in a way that could be embarrassing to her. Alicia would need to offer Mia alternatives and might need to limit access to messy activities for all of the children so that Mia would not feel excluded.

Another thing that Alicia needs to do in this situation is help Ellie understand the value of sensory play. It is possible that the mother does not know the purpose of the activities or how a young child can benefit from them. Alicia can describe how children learn from sensory experiences, acknowledge Mia's creativity, and document her adventures in messy sensory art in order to explain the import learning that takes place during the activities. Alicia could also share some ways that other families handle evening cleanup.

A strong case could be made for both alternatives in this situation, and either position could be justified. Alicia's decision would ultimately be based on the success of her efforts at ethical finesse and her assessment of the specifics of the situation, including how much Mia was benefiting from sensory activities, how she might react to being excluded from them, and how important it was to build trust with her mother. This situation lends itself very well to ethical finesse. And because it is not likely that a child will be seriously harmed from having messy experiences limited, it might make the most sense in this situation to honor Ellie's wishes.

Whatever Alicia decides to do, the Code emphasizes the importance of communication between home and school. A successful resolution to this situation will be more likely if Alicia works hard to understand Ellie's perspective and to ensure that Ellie knew she was listening and willing to work with her. Awareness of the updated NAEYC Code, with its new emphasis on the quality of relationships between teachers and families, may help early childhood educators do a better job of considering parents' needs and involving them in the decisions regarding their children.

> If you were in Alicia's situation, what would you do? Is compromise between what the family wants and what Alicia thinks is best for children one of the solutions you came up with in your brainstorming? Is it possible, and what would make it work? What could Alicia say to Ellie in this situation to communicate her respect and willingness to work collaboratively?

Policy implications. A program could reduce the likelihood of a "messy play" situation like this one arising by providing a new parent orientation that included a demonstration of all of the types of activities offered to the children and the developmental rationale for them. The session could include listening to parents' concerns and discussing possible problems and solutions. School policies and the family handbook could also address the benefit of sensory play for children and guidelines for their participation in it. They could even include some suggestions about things families can do to make it easier to keep children clean (provide a change of clothing, use big shirts as smocks, tie back long hair, etc.).

Reflection on complex-client cases

In our professional ethics workshops, teachers often explore what they should do when they receive requests from family members that run counter to what they think is best for children. Many of the situations in early childhood programs that involve ethical responsibilities to families are similar to the nap and messy play cases presented in this chapter. A related issue involves family members who are concerned about their child's readiness for future school success and ask for more rigorous academic content in preschool or kindergarten. Although the situations vary, all of them can be addressed using the process described in this chapter.

A critical component of dealing successfully with a complex-client situation is the teacher's ability to listen, communicate effectively, and work collaboratively with family members. A competent early childhood educator will make every effort to understand the family's point of view and to accommodate their wishes whenever it is feasible to do so.

Every complex-client case is different, so the final outcome will always depend on the particulars of the situation. In every case it is imperative that the teacher begin by considering whether honoring the parent's request could result in harm to the child. With regard to the two cases presented here, it is more likely that harm to the child would occur in the nap situation because Timothy would be deprived of a basic physiological need. We have presented this case many times, and those who have addressed it have always agreed unanimously (although after long deliberation) that "the ethical early childhood educator" should deny the mother's request if she is convinced that honoring it would be harmful to the child.

The messy play situation described here lends itself better to the use of ethical finesse. There are many things that a teacher could do in this situation to reach an amicable resolution with the parent. Ethical finesse will often get an early childhood educator a happy ending to what looks like a difficult issue. But it may require compromise and receptivity to change on both sides.

Taking the concerns of family members seriously does not mean that a teacher should agree to every request made by a family member without considering its impact on the child. Teachers of young children are professionals who have received training in child development and early childhood care and education. Part of the role they have been educated to play is to help families better understand their young children. The teacher's role in family education is spelled out in the Code.

> I-2.8—To help family members enhance their understanding of their children, as staff are enhancing their understanding of each child through communications with families, and support family members in the continuing development of their skills as parents.

Work in early childhood programs often involves finding a balance between respecting the wishes of families and ensuring that children's needs are met. If teachers are respectful of family members and build good relationships with them from the beginning, these family members will feel better when they learn that all of their requests cannot be accommodated.

The ideal situation in early childhood programs is that teachers and families work in partnership to support children's development and learning. Doing this requires some effort in the best of circumstances, but it can be especially challenging when teachers and family members bring different cultural styles, values, and traditions to their relationships. These differences may take the form of diverse communication styles (verbal and nonverbal) and different expectations for child and adult behavior in a variety of situations. Teachers of young children need to be sensitive to cultural differences and develop skills in working with people from a variety of cultural backgrounds.

Have you faced a situation in which family members wanted you to teach in ways that you didn't believe were best for their children? What strategies and solutions did you use?

Case 6: Culturally based parental practices (Child Abuse Situation II)

For several years, Annette has successfully taught first grade in a neighborhood where many of the residents come from a culture that is different from the one in which she was raised. Her efforts to learn the culture from her students and their parents are appreciated. She has a wonderful reputation and rapport. Annette has a particularly good working relationship with the father of one happy and apparently well-adjusted boy in her class. One day the boy's father shares in a parent meeting that he regularly hits his child with a belt to keep him in line and teach him respect for his elders. Soon after hearing this remark, Annette sees signs of welts on the child's back and legs that could have been left by a belt.

Determine the nature of the problem. This case examines the cultural component of suspected child abuse. It is based on a case discussed in *Young Children* (NAEYC Ethics Panel 1998). It is similar to the child abuse case discussed in Chapter 1 and many of the same considerations apply to it. However, it expands the discussion from a primary focus on the responsibility to the child to take into account the relationship with a parent whose assumptions about appropriate childrearing may be quite different from the teacher's and from community norms as expressed in child abuse laws. Annette recognizes that cultural differences about appropriate discipline for young children may be central to this matter. But this realization does not keep her from being troubled by what she regards as possible abusive treatment of the child. In this situation, as in any situation that involves the suspicion of abuse, Annette must weigh her responsibility for protecting the child's well-being with her commitment to maintaining a respectful relationship with his father and honoring his cultural attitudes about parenting. The question she faces is, "What definition of abuse will serve the best interest of this child and avoid unwarranted interference with his family's childrearing practices?"

Consider ethical finesse. This dilemma poses a particular challenge because Annette enjoys a good relationship with the father and the child is doing well in school. At this point Annette deeply regrets not having given all parents of children in her class information about the nature and consequences of child abuse at the beginning of the school year. She also wishes she had turned the occasion of the father's first comment into an opportunity for him and for other families to understand the consequences of harsh corporal punishment. In cases involving child abuse, resolutions cannot be finessed once the suspicion of abuse is planted. There is no turning back from confronting it. Annette must seek the fine line of distinction between abuse and culturally diverse approaches to discipline.

Look for guidance in the Code. The Core Values of the NAEYC Code remind Annette of her commitments to support children's development, to honor the bond between child and family, to respect diversity, and to respect individuals, but they but don't directly address a situation that involves abuse of a child. Guidance for addressing these circumstances can be found in the Code's Ideals and Principles.

The most relevant Ideal is

I-1.4—To appreciate the vulnerability of children. . . .

Applicable Principles are

P-1.1—Above all, we shall not harm children. We shall not participate in practices that are emotionally damaging [or] physically harmful . . . to children. *This principle has precedence over all others in this Code.*

P-1.8—We shall be familiar with the risk factors for and symptoms of child abuse and neglect, including physical, sexual, verbal, and emotional abuse and physical, emotional, educational, and medical neglect. We shall know and follow state laws and community procedures that protect children against abuse and neglect.

P-1.9—When we have reasonable cause to suspect child abuse or neglect, we shall report it to the appropriate community agency and follow up to ensure that appropriate action has been taken. When appropriate, parents or guardians will be informed that the referral will be or has been made.

Annette also pays special attention to the Ideals that remind her of early childhood educators' responsibilities to families, including

I-2.2—To develop relationships of mutual trust and create partnerships with the families we serve.

I-2.5—To respect the dignity and preferences of each family and to make an effort to learn about its structure, culture, language, customs, and beliefs to ensure a culturally consistent environment for all children and families.

I-2.6—To acknowledge families' childrearing values and their right to make decisions for their children.

She also considers the following principle:

P-2.2—We shall inform families of program philosophy [and] policies . . . which should be in accordance with our ethical responsibilities to children.

Before she can make any decision, Annette realizes that she needs more information. If the father's and the child's responses to her polite inquiries convince Annette that her concerns are unfounded, she will not take any action but will be watchful for incidents that could create a reason for concern.

When Annette's inquiries make clear that the father has indeed hit his son with a belt, she knows she has a legal and an ethical responsibility as spelled out in the Code and community statutes to follow mandated reporting laws. She feels that the boy is not in imminent danger, and she wants to make every possible effort to maintain a positive relationship with the father.

When Cultural Perspectives Differ

Conflicts between parents and teachers arise because even though conscientious adults want to do the right thing, their assumptions, values, and aspirations for children are not always the same. Sometimes these differences reflect cultural perspectives.

Gonzalez-Mena (2008) poses this contrast as an example: Americans with a Northern European background typically stress the importance of developing children's "internal locus of control," while Hispanic and African Americans are more likely to rely on the eyes and ears of the entire community to monitor children's behavior.

Gonzalez-Mena also observes that a number of arenas exist in which cultural differences can generate issues with families in programs for young children. These include differences in how those from various cultures socialize children to be part of a group, how they view the desirability of personal possessions, how they look upon competition among children, and how they administer discipline.

Lilian Katz also emphasizes the importance of being aware of cultural perspectives. She observes that practitioners may "reflect and cherish middle-class values and tend to confuse conventional behavior with normal development" (1991, 8). This observation reminds early childhood educators that it is important to identify the cultural biases they bring to their work with young children and make concerted efforts to assume inclusive attitudes as they interact with children and families. People who work with young children need to be alert to how they can honor and support different perspectives and help children become successful in both their home and school surroundings.

Success in these efforts often depends on effective communication. It is important, for example, to observe how individuals from various cultures use personal space; when they smile, touch, and make eye contact with each other; and how they define being on time. All of these behaviors vary across cultures, and well-intentioned behavior can be misinterpreted if cultural differences are not taken into account. In Western cultures, for example, looking an authority figure in the eye is a sign of respect, but to many Native Americans this behavior would be considered rude (Gonzalez-Mena 2008). Learning to read individuals' body language as well as their words can help a teacher avoid many misunderstandings and overcome any number of problems.

The importance of cultural sensitivity has been increasingly emphasized in the field of early childhood education. NAEYC's influential position statement "Developmentally

Decide on a course of action. Annette meets with the father to explain that child protection laws in their community do not permit harsh corporal punishment, usually defined as having left a mark. She tells him that, as much as it troubles her to do so, she is required by law and by professional ethical guidelines to report the evident child abuse. Annette hopes that the child protective services agency will recognize that he is a committed and involved father and will only require that he take parenting classes.

Appropriate Practice in Early Childhood Programs Serving Children from Birth through Age 8" (NAEYC 2009) emphasizes the importance of cultural, in addition to age and individual, appropriateness as a key consideration in making decisions about the education and care of young children.

The Pathways to Cultural Competence Project (NAEYC 2010) is designed to assist educators in supporting diversity in early childhood programs. This effort, based on input and thinking from experts and the field at large, has four underlying principles designed to assist teachers in working with diverse families:

1. Teacher reflection that focuses on how values and practices regarding children's learning are influenced by the cultural and linguistic background of teachers and administrators.

2. Intentional decision making and practice that focuses on identifying shared childrearing goals with families and aligning program decision making and policies with these shared goals.

3. A strength-based perspective that acknowledges that programs can learn from families and recognizes that diversity enriches and provides depth to the overall program.

4. Open, ongoing two-way communication between programs and families. This principle is intended to ensure that families have opportunities to give input to program policies and practices.

Early childhood educators have, in recent years, dedicated themselves to ensuring that young children's and families' educational experiences reflect the rich mosaic of cultures that make up the United States. We have come to appreciate that there is not one "right way" to care for and educate young children. Cultural beliefs and values permeate every interaction between children and adults, and between the adults who work with young children. It is our responsibility as early childhood educators to learn about the families and communities we serve so that our work with children will prepare them for success in their home communities and beyond.

Do you work with families whose cultures are different from your own? What cultural differences have created special challenges for you? How do you negotiate the issues that arise?

Annette realizes that the NAEYC Code backs her decision, telling her that she must act in ways that are right rather than ways that are comfortable or popular. Knowledge of her ethical obligations helps Annette have the courage to report this situation.

Policy implications. Janet Gonzalez-Mena, in addressing the difficult issues involved in assessing child abuse in cross-cultural situations, offers the following advice:

> You're bound by law to report suspected physical abuse (physical punishment that leaves marks on the child). Be sure parents know this from the start so they won't feel betrayed if you have to report suspected abuse. . . . Be respectful of their differing beliefs, but clear about the law. (2008, 139)

Providing parent education, developing policies regarding the center's obligation to watch for and report suspected child abuse, and sharing policies with all families helps in situations involving corporal punishment. Family members may modify the ways they discipline children when they become aware of community definitions of child abuse and teachers' obligations when they see evidence of abuse. Had these practices been implemented in this situation, the issue of a referral for child abuse might not have arisen.

Do you agree with Annette's decision to report the possible child abuse by this father? Should exceptions to the NAEYC Code be made when cultural differences in child discipline exist between the early childhood program and the family? What philosophical principles could you use to justify your answer to this question?

6

Ethical Responsibilities to Colleagues

In a caring, cooperative workplace, human dignity is respected, profes-
sional satisfaction is promoted, and positive relationships are developed
and sustained. Based upon our core values, our primary responsibility
to colleagues is to establish and maintain settings and relationships
that support productive work and meet professional needs. The same
ideals that apply to children also apply as we interact with adults in the
workplace.[1]

—NAEYC Code of Ethical Conduct and Statement of Commitment

The third section of the NAEYC Code of Ethical Conduct focuses on the relationships among the adults in early care and education settings and spells out early childhood professionals' ethical obligations to coworkers and employers. This section of the Code is based on the premise that supportive and collegial work environments are good for early childhood educators and enhance their ability to provide high-quality education and care for children.

---

[1]This section of the Code addresses our responsibilities to coworkers and to employers. See the *Code of Ethical Conduct: Supplement for Early Childhood Program Administrators* for responsibilities to personnel.

Ideals

The Code's six Ideals relating to our ethical responsibilities to coworkers and employers tell us that we should aspire to establish and maintain positive relationships with the adults in our workplace by honoring confidences while being respectful, trustworthy, and collaborative. They also create the expectation that we will provide high-quality services that enhance the reputation of the setting in which we work. In the 2005 revision of the Code, I-3A.1 was modified to emphasize the importance of confidentiality and collaboration in relationships with colleagues, and I-3A.2 was revised to clarify that the goal of sharing resources with coworkers is to provide the best possible early childhood care and education program. See the chart showing Code revisions in the Appendix.

Principles

The nine Principles (or rules of professional conduct) in this section of the Code address our ethical responsibilities to coworkers and employers. The items concerning our responsibilities to coworkers call on us to recognize colleagues' contributions while avoiding doing anything that could diminish their reputation or detract from their effectiveness, to express opinions and share concerns about the performance of a coworker with that person confidentially, and to avoid discriminatory practices. With regard to employers, the Code emphasizes our obligations to follow program policies, speak and act on behalf of the setting only when authorized to do so, and to follow laws and regulations designed to protect children. The 2005 revision added a new principle, P-3A.1, that addresses recognizing colleagues' contributions and not participating in practices that diminish their reputations or impair their effectiveness. Principle P-3A.2 was modified to make the point that efforts to resolve concerns about the professional behavior of a coworker should be conducted in a confidential manner. Item P-3B.4, relating to responsibilities to employers, was modified to highlight that concerns with the behavior of a colleague should be handled collegially unless children's well-being is at stake. A new item, P-3B.5, requires employees to inform program administration or other authorities when they have concerns about conditions that impact the quality of care and education in a program.

Typical ethical dilemmas involving colleagues

Surveys conducted in the United States and Australia indicate that early childhood educators frequently encounter ethical dilemmas concerning their relationships with colleagues. The following situations were mentioned as being of particular concern: hearing a colleague discuss a child or family outside of the program or school setting, observing a colleague disciplining children very harshly, observing colleagues providing activities for children that are not worthwhile or appropriate, having colleagues leave the classroom to conduct personal business, being required to implement policies that are not good for children, and experiencing unfair employment practices (Feeney & Sysko 1986; Rodd & Clyde 1991).

The pages that follow present five dilemmas that highlight early childhood educators' ethical responsibilities to colleagues. Each case involves mixed obligations—a conflict between what an early childhood educator believes is in the best interests of children, families, or the community and what she believes will preserve a good relationship with one or more colleagues. Each case calls for the person involved to make a decision about which of the conflicting obligations should be accorded the greatest weight. Specific sections of the Code applied to each case help us think about what we must do, what we can do, and what we cannot do as we consider defensible resolutions to these kinds of frequently occurring workplace situations.

Case 7: Personal business

Barbara and her coteacher, Vanessa, work with a group of 20 4-year-olds (two of whom have special needs) in an inclusive inner-city child development center. Their classroom is a portable building, one of six units clustered around a small, central courtyard. Several times recently Vanessa has stepped into a corner of the room and turned away from the children for periods of up to 30 minutes to text on her cell phone.

> What is your first reaction to this case? To whom does Barbara have obligations? What considerations should she take into account in deciding what to do? What actions might she take?

What should the ethical early childhood educator do?

Barbara knows that program staff are responsible for supervising all the children in their care at all times. The dilemma that exists from her perspective involves ensuring children's safety and maintaining the program's quality without jeopardizing the good relationship she has with her coteacher.

Determine the nature of the problem. Barbara quickly realizes this situation involves ethics because it revolves around her responsibilities to the children in her care, their families, and her employer. She knows she cannot turn a blind eye when her colleague's lack of attention could put the children at risk. Failing to act would be in violation of her responsibility to assist the program in providing the best possible services to the children entrusted in its care.

> Have you experienced a situation in which a coworker did not meet her responsibilities? What did you do? Was the resolution satisfactory?

Consider ethical finesse. The first time Vanessa turns her attention away from the children, she explains to Barbara that it was an emergency and won't happen again. The second time Vanessa texts for a long time, Barbara realizes that she must address Vanessa's behavior without delay. She spends some time thinking about how to communicate her concerns to Vanessa in a respectful and nonaccusatory way. She says to Vanessa, "I know that you had to take care of a personal issue during class time again today. Is everything OK? Is there anything I can do to help you out?"

Barbara points out calmly that it is difficult for one person alone to handle the whole group and that she worries about the children's safety and the quality of their experiences. She reminds Vanessa of how critical it is to have an appropriate ratio of attentive adults to children at all times. She suggests that if Vanessa must turn her attention away from the children that she ask the director or someone in the office to take her place in the classroom so that she can leave the room.

Barbara hopes that being straightforward with Vanessa about her concerns will enable her to see the effects of her behavior on the program and the potential risks she creates for the children. In addition, their discussion could motivate Vanessa to find a better time to deal with personal matters.

Look for guidance in the Code. Once it has become clear that her efforts have not led Vanessa to change her behavior, Barbara consults the NAEYC Code to gain some insight into how she might address this situation.

She recognizes that these Core Values help her identify the dilemma she is facing:

- Respect the dignity, worth, and uniqueness of each individual (child, family member, and colleague)
- Recognize that children and adults achieve their full potential in the context of relationships that are based on trust and respect

Her review of the Code begins with the first section that describes her obligations to children:

> I-1.5—To create and maintain safe and healthy settings that foster children's social, emotional, cognitive, and physical development and that respect their dignity and their contributions.

She also realizes Principle 1.1, "Above all, we shall not harm children," could apply. She does not think that any harm has come to the children as a result of Vanessa's inattention, but she is concerned that she would not be able handle an emergency, if one occurred, while supervising a group of 20 children virtually alone.

Barbara next turns to Section III of the Code, which addresses her responsibilities to colleagues, and finds these items that address her responsibilities to coworkers:

> I-3A.1—To establish and maintain relationships of respect, trust, confidentiality, collaboration, and cooperation with coworkers.

> P-3A.2—When we have concerns about the professional behavior of a coworker, we shall first let that person know of our concern in a way that shows respect for personal dignity and for the diversity to be found among staff members, and then attempt to resolve the matter collegially and in a confidential manner.

Barbara also realizes that, since it is not possible to provide high-quality service when both teachers are not fully engaged with the children, she is not able to meet the responsibility she has to her employer when Vanessa is texting:

> I-3B.1—To assist the program in providing the highest quality of service.

And finally, Barbara notes that she would be justified in taking this issue to the director if Vanessa's performance does not improve. These principles would justify that course of action if it were necessary:

> P-3B.3—We shall not violate laws or regulations designed to protect children and shall take appropriate action consistent with this Code when aware of such violations.

> P-3B.4—If we have concerns about a colleague's behavior, and children's well-being is not at risk, we may address the concern with that individual. If children are at risk or the situation does not improve after it has been brought to the colleague's attention, we shall report the colleague's unethical or incompetent behavior to an appropriate authority.

> P-3B.5—When we have a concern about circumstances or conditions that impact the quality of care and education within the program, we shall inform the program's administration. . . .

Decide on a course of action. In many situations a colleague approached in this way would recognize the possible consequences of her behavior and would avoid being distracted in the future. In other instances the coworker may become defensive and unyielding about the behavior being questioned. Barbara knows that if the latter happens, she will need to find another course of action.

Soon after their discussion, Vanessa is again preoccupied with personal issues and is on her phone for half an hour. She gives no explanation for her behavior. Barbara can't help feeling resentful because of the potentially dangerous situation that Vanessa is creating. Once more she tries to reach out, asking Vanessa if she is feeling unwell or facing a personal situation that can only be addressed at a particular time of day. Vanessa says she is sorry but offers no explanation.

Vanessa repeats her behavior again a few days later. Based on the Code's guidance regarding relationships with coworkers, Barbara makes another good-faith effort to reach a collegial resolution. Again she expresses her concerns about the safety issues involved when one person must supervise 20 children without assistance. She urges Vanessa to find a better time to conduct personal business and points out that if this behavior persists that she will have to share her concern with the director. Vanessa says she understands and promises it won't happen again.

Two weeks later Vanessa once more turns her back to text without an explanation. Because the children's safety is at risk and her attempts at a collegial resolution have been unsuccessful, Barbara reports what has been happening to the program director. The director discusses the urgency of the situation with Vanessa, who shares with the director that she has a personal issue that requires her frequent attention. The director emphasizes to Vanessa the need for her to devote full attention to the children while "on duty."

Policy implications. It's likely that the program's staff manual reminds employees that they must maintain the adult-to-child ratios required by licensing at all times; failing to do so jeopardizes the program's good standing with the licensing agency. In this instance Vanessa is complying with the letter of the law, but is not fully available to supervise and interact appropriately with children. With applicable policies in place, the program administrator is responsible for monitoring compliance and promptly addressing any lapses that occur.

> Can you think of any other approaches Barbara could have used to persuade Vanessa to meet her professional obligations? Do you believe Barbara was justified in telling the director that Vanessa had been distracted and inattentive? Do you think it was easy for Barbara to do this? What would you have done in this situation?

Case 8: Teacher talk

Natasha, a second grade teacher; Gail, the Title I resource teacher; Deborah, the teacher in the room next to Natasha's; and several others gather in the staff room, preparing class materials and drinking coffee. Natasha and Gail have learned this morning that the father of Dennis, a child in Natasha's class with whom Gail works on a regular basis, moved out of the house he lived in with Dennis and his mother.

"What's the matter with Dennis today?" asks Deborah. "He is a terror. Every time I see him on the playground, he is picking a fight with another child."

"It's not surprising," says Gail, "You won't believe what his father did this time. Dennis's mother told Natasha and me this morning."

Gail proceeds to relate all of the details that she heard about the fight between Dennis's parents that led to his father packing his clothes and storming out of the house.

> What is your reaction to the situation described here? Does Natasha have any obligations and to whom? What should she consider in deciding what to do? Brainstorm some actions she could take in this situation.

What should the ethical early childhood educator do?

A number of cases dealing with the management of personal information were reported in NAEYC ethics surveys. Some cases involved families wanting information about other children in their child's class. In one situation parents wanted the name of the child in a toddler group who bit their daughter; in another case a volunteer wanted to know which children came from families who were on welfare. Other situations such as this one involve staff members inappropriately sharing privileged information about children and families.

Determine the nature of the problem. This case is similar to the earlier situation in which a teacher has to consider how to respond when her colleague neglects her professional responsibilities. In this instance Natasha has to respond to Gail, who has failed to live up to her ethical responsibility to protect this family's privacy. Natasha, who witnesses this breach of confidentiality, needs to sort out her obligations to the family of a child in her class and to the resource teacher who is her colleague and friend. Her desire to meet both obligations has created an ethical dilemma.

For one thing, Natasha fears that someone might unwittingly mention what they have heard to Dennis's mother and damage both teachers' relationships with her. On the other hand, Natasha knows that gossip is a fact of life in many schools. It happens all the time, is not likely to go away, and usually doesn't cause any harm. In fact, Gail may think that sharing this information helps other teachers who come into contact with Dennis in the course of the day to be more accepting of his behavior during this stressful period.

What Natasha needs to consider in this situation is how to help her coworker understand that she shouldn't gossip about families—it breaches her ethical responsibilities and can damage her working relationship with families and colleagues. Natasha wants to help Gail become more sensitive to her obligation to hold privileged information in confidence.

Consider ethical finesse. This situation lends itself well to ethical finesse. Natasha has a good relationship with Gail so she gently and respectfully reminds her of the early childhood educator's professional responsibility to keep privileged information confidential. She says, "Gail, I'm not comfortable hearing talk about private family matters. I wouldn't want anyone sharing such personal information about me." She hopes such a simple reminder is enough to lead Gail and nearby colleagues into other school talk and away from gossip.

Natasha also mentally rehearses other points she could make if Gail or other teachers persist in indiscriminately sharing personal information. She realizes that having a copy of the Code handy could be helpful to illustrate that the admonition of "don't gossip" comes from an important Principle that guides all early childhood educators, not just her own opinion or preference.

Look for guidance in the Code. Like Barbara in the previous case, Natasha is guided by two of the Code's Core Values: "Respect the dignity, worth, and uniqueness of each individual" and "Recognize that children and adults achieve their full potential in the context of relationships that are based on trust and respect."

Even though this situation involves Natasha's relationship with her colleagues, she begins by referring to Section II of the Code, which addresses our responsibilities to families. She finds the two items listed below that help guide her decision making. She is particularly glad to see item P-2.13, which explicitly addresses the situation she is currently facing.

I-2.2—To develop relationships of mutual trust and create partnerships with the families we serve.

P-2.13—We shall maintain confidentiality and shall respect the family's right to privacy, refraining from disclosure of confidential information and intrusion into family life. . . .

Natasha then turns to the third section of the Code, which addresses her responsibilities to coworkers, for guidance about how to respond to Gail. She finds that the same two items that guided Barbara's thinking in the case described above can also help her:

I-3A.1—To establish and maintain relationships of respect [and] trust . . . with coworkers.

P-3A.2—When we have concerns about the professional behavior of a coworker, we shall first let that person know of our concern. . . .

It is helpful to think about how these items apply to Natasha's dilemma, just as they applied to the situation faced by Barbara in the previous case in this chapter. In that instance Barbara had time to refer to the Code and plan her course of action, but Natasha needs to respond to this situation immediately and is not likely to have time to consult the Code. She cannot listen to idle gossip without appearing to condone it. News can spread quickly through some schools, and if Natasha wants to make sure this story isn't repeated, she should respond when she hears the gossip. One reason it is so important for early childhood educators to be familiar with the Code is that they often need to respond quickly to a situation.

Decide on a course of action. If efforts to finesse this situation are not successful, then Natasha must consider alternate actions. The next week Natasha overhears Gail relating the story of the family fight to a volunteer who has commented on Dennis's disruptive behavior. Her colleague's continuing disregard for a family's privacy troubles Natasha. She realizes that an ethical early childhood educator should not stand by and allow destructive gossip to continue.

Natasha doesn't want to make the situation into such a big issue that it jeopardizes her good relationship with Gail. She decides to chat informally with the school principal and mention her concern about confidential information being discussed inappropriately. She expresses her concern in a general way and does not mention names. The principal says that she will bring the topic up at the next staff meeting and also look into having an ethics workshop for the entire staff in the near future.

Natasha's problem is one many early childhood educators face. It can be difficult to make a distinction between legitimate teacher talk and idle gossip. In the case of Dennis's family, for example, it might be appropriate for Gail to give her colleagues general information, such as "Dennis's family is going through a difficult time, and his behavior might show that he is under stress." She crossed the line, however, by sharing all the details of what she heard. It is appropriate to tell colleagues facts they need to know to meet a child's needs, but we must be very mindful not to betray confidences or share sensitive information indiscriminately.

Does Natasha's decision to talk collegially with Gail make sense in this situation? Is there anything else that she could have done to discourage Gail's disclosure of confidential information? How does the NAEYC Code support her decision? Have you worked with someone who inappropriately shared confidential information about children and families? How did you handle the situation?

Policy implications. All early childhood educators need to know that maintaining confidentiality (not sharing information obtained in professional practice, except under clearly defined circumstances) is an essential moral commitment of every profession. Honoring the ethical commitment to confidentiality is particularly important in early childhood settings because we often know a great deal of personal information about children and their families.

Natasha may have more easily dealt with this situation if she could have referred to clear, current school policies that were well known to everyone who works in the program—teachers, support staff, administrators, and families. Also, if the program had established in writing that NAEYC's Code of Ethical Conduct would be followed, this dilemma might not have occurred or could more easily be resolved. One respondent to NAEYC surveys described the Code as "a tool that helps dissolve unethical practices" (NAEYC Ethics Panel 1994b, 51).

Policies Regarding Confidentiality

Confidentiality is more easily maintained when programs and schools establish policies regarding how information should be handled. Consider these sample guidelines, grounded firmly in the Code, that may help programs in formulating policies to address the question, "Who needs to know?"

- We will not disclose personal information (such as address, economic status, health status, or family structure) about children or families to other families or those outside the school without permission from a family member or a court order.

- We will not discuss a child or family in a way that makes their identity obvious when a third party is present or in a public location.

- We will not share sensitive information given to us by a parent without the parent's permission (unless there is a risk to the child).

- Information shared with staff should be limited to what they need to know to provide quality services for children.

- All staff members should be made aware of confidentiality guidelines.

Case 9: Difficult separations

Whenever Aaron's mother leaves him at his child care center, the 3-year-old expresses his feelings about the separation through aggressive behavior toward the other children. Pat, the assistant teacher in Aaron's room, is dismayed by the way Sylvia, the lead teacher, responds to his behavior. Sylvia makes Aaron sit on a stool for long periods of time. Pat believes that Sylvia's response should be constructive and reflect an understanding of the circumstance triggering the misbehavior. Pat wants to give Aaron a safe outlet for expressing his feelings, such as pounding clay or redirecting his energy in positive ways.

> What is your first reaction? To whom does Pat have obligations? What things should she take into consideration in deciding what to do? Think about some things she could do to resolve this situation.

What should the ethical early childhood educator do?

This case and the others presented in this chapter involve an early childhood educator trying to balance the best interest of a child with her relationship with a colleague. The focus in this instance is on classroom management. This case was first published in *Young Children,* and responses from readers are incorporated in the following discussion (NAEYC Ethics Panel 1994a).

Determine the nature of the problem. The central issue in this situation is Pat's responsibility when she believes that her colleague's response to a child's disruptive behavior is excessively harsh. Pat is concerned about Aaron, but she needs to work with Sylvia every day so she knows that it is important to maintain a collegial relationship with her. She finds her situation particularly stressful and awkward because it is the lead teacher who is not providing this child the positive guidance he needs. Pat wants to respect her superior, but she knows it is not appropriate to ignore a practice that may be harming a child.

Consider ethical finesse. Pat wishes she could ignore the situation, but she realizes that for Aaron's sake she must do something. The NAEYC Code supports her inclination to deal with the problem collegially. She arranges to meet with Sylvia after school and explains her concern about Aaron. Pat shares with Sylvia an article she has read recently about handling transitions.

She suggests she would like for them to try some of the techniques described there, which might make Aaron's arrival at school go more smoothly. One recommendation is to involve his mother in the separation routine, and another suggests giving Aaron more one-on-one attention upon his arrival.

Certainly the most desirable outcome to this dilemma would be for Sylvia to see for herself that her strategy for guiding children's behavior is not working and be willing to try a different approach to help Aaron to make the transition to school. Pat wisely realizes that Sylvia may find changing her approach more palatable if she can attribute her decision to a professional resource rather than to her assistant's advice.

Sylvia's reaction to Pat's suggestion is likely to depend on their relationship and the way that decisions about child guidance are made in their program. In any event, it's a good habit for teaching teams to share resources. This practice helps create shared views and builds teachers' feelings of professionalism and competence.

Look for guidance in the Code. The Code's Core Values are again a good place to begin analyzing this case. Sylvia's thinking is guided by the two items we have relied on to find a resolution to the cases above: "Respect the dignity, worth, and uniqueness of each individual" and "Recognize that children and adults achieve their full potential in the context of relationships that are based on trust and respect." She believes one additional Core Value also applies to this case: "Base our work on knowledge of how children develop and learn."

When Pat consults the Code, she realizes this case involves both her responsibilities to children as well as to her colleagues. Turning to the first section of the Code she finds that in addition to P-1.1, "Above all, we shall not harm children," these Ideals and Principles apply:

I-1.2—To base program practices upon current knowledge and research in the field of early childhood education, child development, and related disciplines, as well as on particular knowledge of each child.

I-1.4—To appreciate the vulnerability of children and their dependence on adults.

I-1.5—To create and maintain safe and healthy settings that foster children's social, emotional, cognitive, and physical development and that respect their dignity and their contributions.

She also notes Section III of the Code, which addresses her responsibilities to coworkers, can guide her thinking, as it did for Barbara and Natasha in the cases above. She finds guidance in the following:

I-3A.1—To establish and maintain relationships of respect [and] trust . . . with coworkers.

I-3A.2—To share resources with coworkers. . . .

P-3A.2—When we have concerns about the professional behavior of a coworker, we shall first let that person know of our concern. . . .

I-3B.1—To assist the program in providing the highest quality of service.

P-3B.4—If we have concerns about a colleague's behavior, and children's well-being is not at risk, we may address the concern with that individual. If children are at risk or the situation does not improve after it has been brought to the colleague's attention, we shall report the colleague's unethical or incompetent behavior to an appropriate authority.

Decide on a course of action. When Pat's overtures to Sylvia are repeatedly ignored or rejected, she realizes that her attempts at ethical finesse are not going to be successful. She knows that there is no justification for the way Sylvia is handling Aaron's morning outbursts.

Pat decides she must try talking to Sylvia again to express even more strongly her concerns about the possible negative consequences of her colleague's actions. When these discussions do not produce any change, Pat feels she must do something to protect the child.

Pat is reluctant to discuss this problem with the center director, because doing so would likely permanently damage her relationship with Sylvia. She is tempted to quietly do what she can to help Aaron without attracting Sylvia's disapproval. After more soul searching, however, she decides that her obligation to Aaron must override these concerns. She discusses Sylvia's behavior and her concern for Aaron's welfare with her program director and knows that taking this step is supported in the Code, specifically by item P-3B.4.

Policy implications. Policies that include guidelines describing appropriate approaches to guidance and discipline might have prevented this dilemma. More importantly, however, the director should be circulating throughout the center on a regular and ongoing basis. If she were, she would have observed this inappropriate discipline approach and could have stepped in immediately, eliminating the difficult situation Pat found herself navigating.

> What makes a difference of opinion about strategies for guiding children's behavior an ethical dilemma? Under what circumstances do you think a director should become involved? Should the fact that Sylvia is Pat's supervisor have affected her decision to speak to the director about her concerns? Have you faced a situation in which a colleague treated a child in a way you didn't like? What did you do? How did you justify it? How can Pat use ethical Principles from the Code to justify her decision?

Colleagues' Unprofessional Behavior

The three cases (7, 8, and 9) discussed on preceding pages involve a staff member's concern when a coworker behaves unprofessionally or violates the Code of Ethical Conduct. Other situations early childhood educators report in surveys include hearing a colleague make insulting jokes about children and families of a particular ethnic group, a teacher chronically coming late to work, and a teacher arriving at work unprepared and borrowing lesson plans and materials from others.

An early childhood educator has several possible courses of action when faced with a colleague's unprofessional behavior. First, she can avoid conflict by ignoring the troubling behavior. Because people in the early childhood field are usually concerned with preserving harmonious relationships, they often choose this action. The advantage, of course, is that it will not create any conflict or jeopardize a relationship. The disadvantage is that a colleague who doesn't know someone has a problem with her behavior is unlikely to change it.

A second alternative is that the person with a concern can share it in a diplomatic way with the person whose behavior is troubling. For example, the early childhood educator bothered by the ethnic joke could say, "It makes me uncomfortable when you tell a joke that ridicules children and their families."

Finally, if an individual feels a colleague's professional behavior is potentially harmful to children or damaging to the program (such as the case of the teacher whose coteacher leaves her to supervise a large group of children alone), she should first directly address the person involved. If this does not lead to a positive outcome, then she must report the situation to someone who has the authority to solve the problem.

In most cases the early childhood educator has the option of deciding whether and how to respond. When children's welfare is at stake, the early childhood professional has an obligation to act promptly to protect them.

Case 10: The "pushed-down" curriculum

Steve is delighted to obtain a teaching job that pays well in a child care center in a middle-class suburban neighborhood near his home. He's been told that the center's curriculum addresses the state's voluntary early learning guidelines for preschoolers, and he knows he'll be comfortable addressing them—he has had several years' experience teaching required standards through authentic hands-on experiences. As he begins teaching, it surprises him to find that he is expected to have 3- and 4-year-olds sit still and use workbooks for long periods of time each day. He is told that the daily program should also include drills on the alphabet and counting to 100.

Steve observes that in the other classrooms adults initiate most of the interactions, and children get few opportunities to engage with each other or to work with blocks, play dress-up, or use other appropriate manipulatives. This style of teaching, pushed down from higher grades, conflicts with what Steve knows is appropriate for pre-schoolers. When Steve asks the director and other teachers about the developmental appropriateness of the center's preschool curriculum, they assure him there are no problems. They explain that families are very happy, and the children always do well on the admission tests for prestigious private schools.

How do you react to Steve's situation? To whom does he have obligations? What should he consider in deciding on a course of action? Brainstorm some ways that one could address this situation.

What should the ethical early childhood educator do?

This case, like the previous ones in this chapter, addresses colleagues' behavior and teachers' relationships with their peers, but the focus here is on curriculum. When a situation like Steve's was presented in *Young Children* (Feeney 1987), it focused on a teacher educator rather than the teacher. Responses to that case by readers of *Young Children* are included in the discussion that follows.

Determine the nature of the problem. Steve faces a troubling situation because the center's director and staff rely on educational practices that directly contradict accepted best practices for supporting the development and learning of young children. Steve wants to be a good colleague and employee, but he also feels a strong obligation to teach in ways he believes are best for young children.

Consider ethical finesse. Steve tries a proactive approach to effect change in the center's curriculum. He tells his director about his experience addressing standards using active, hands-on activities, and offers to lead a staff development session on developmentally appropriate practice. Steve also brings in books, articles, and information about websites that describe appropriate teaching approaches to share with the other teachers.

The director and teachers listen politely, but Steve soon realizes they are not interested in what he has to say. They are experienced and comfortable with the way they teach. Moreover, the parents are satisfied with the program because their children are developing the academic skills they know will be important in kindergarten. Steve realizes that the program is not likely to change any time soon.

Look for guidance in the Code. Steve first learned about the NAEYC Code during his preservice education. He has relied on it to help him address difficult situations throughout his teaching career. He refers to it now to help him think through this predicament.

The Core Values that helped Barbara, Natasha, and Pat resolve their dilemmas are again a good place to begin: "Respect the dignity, worth, and uniqueness of each individual"; "Recognize that children and adults achieve their full potential in the context of relationships that are based on trust and respect"; and "Base our work on knowledge of how children develop and learn."

Some of the Ideals and Principles in the Code's sections on responsibilities to children and colleagues that have been helpful to analyze the cases described earlier are also helpful in this instance:

I-1.2—To base program practices upon current knowledge and research in the field. . . .

I-1.5—To create and maintain safe and healthy settings that foster children's social, emotional, cognitive, and physical development. . . .

I-3A.2—To share resources with coworkers. . . .

One additional item applies to Steve's particular circumstances and helps him decide on a defensible course of action. We believe this item can guide Steve's thinking even though the curriculum choice may, strictly speaking, be general practice and not a policy of the center.

P-3B.1—We shall follow all program policies. When we do not agree with program policies, we shall attempt to effect change through constructive action within the organization.

> Have you worked in a setting in which you did not believe the curriculum or teaching strategies were appropriate for the children? What did you do and why? What happened as a result of your actions?

Decide on a course of action. Steve sees that expecting the other teachers to change is unrealistic, and while the program may not be developmentally appropriate, it does not appear to be harming the children. But he realizes that he cannot in good conscience teach in ways that violate his understanding of good practice. He asks the director to allow him to modify the center's typical curriculum and teaching strategies for his group of children.

Steve decides that if he is allowed to teach in ways he believes are appropriate, he will remain in the position and continue to diplomatically advocate for more worthwhile content and hands-on teaching methods. If the director will not allow him to make these changes, he plans to look for employment in a setting more congruent with his educational philosophy.

Policy implications. Programs of early care and education adopt a wide range of approaches to implementing a curriculum. It is important to learn about the program's approach to curriculum and to consider the match between any mandated curriculum and your professional knowledge of best practices. As you prepare to accept any teaching position, you should also learn about how much autonomy teachers have. Your goal should be to avoid putting yourself in a position where teaching the way you know is best would be a violation of your employer's expectations.

> Do you think a teacher should work in a setting where the teaching methods and curriculum are at odds with current knowledge of child development and best practice, as he understands them? What are your thoughts about Steve's decision to stay in his job if he is allowed to teach in his own way?

Case 11: The "fun" curriculum (a variation of Case 10)

Hana has found that many of the activities presented to toddlers and 2-year-olds in her center are pointless and do not support their development in any meaningful way. She is uncomfortable that her coteachers often develop themes and offer activities that are trivial, such as cartoon character coloring pages, preparing craft projects that result in identical finished products, dancing to popular music with lyrics more suitable for high school students than toddlers, and painting with chocolate pudding.

The other teachers maintain that activities that are fun for them are also fun for the children, and that is enough justification for doing them. Hana believes that any planned activity must have a developmental purpose, be meaningful to children, and be appropriate for their age level.

What should the ethical early childhood educator do?

This case, like the previous one, involves early childhood curriculum; a variation of this case was first discussed in *Young Children* (NAEYC Ethics Panel 1994c). Hana, like Steve, is convinced her colleagues's teaching approach is not harming children, although it is not helping them to develop as they would through a more appropriate curriculum. Like Steve, she decides that the best way to address her concern is to help her colleagues gain a better understanding of child development by modeling developmentally appropriate practice. She also plans to bring in articles about best practices and offer to invite a local expert to give a curriculum workshop at the program.

This variation and the previous dilemma represent the two extremes of an early childhood curriculum continuum. At one end is the approach "pushed down" from higher grades that overemphasizes teaching academic content using developmentally inappropriate strategies that are too rigid, fragmented, and unsuited to the way that young children learn best. On the other end is a haphazard, trivialized, or merely "fun" approach that lacks substance and intellectual integrity. Between these two extremes lie more balanced curricular approaches that reflect what we know about child development and how children learn best. These are the approaches the early childhood profession calls *developmentally appropriate.*

The research base of early childhood education

Several cases presented in this chapter raise basic questions about early childhood educators' practice: What are the best strategies for teaching young children? What is appropriate curriculum content? How should we guide young children's behavior?

These questions take us first to the Code, where we find one related Core Value as well as two Ideals in Section I that address our responsibilities to children:

Core Value:

> • Base our work on knowledge of how children develop and learn

Ideals:

> I-1.1—To be familiar with the knowledge base of early childhood care and education and to stay informed through continuing education and training.
>
> I-1.2—To base program practices upon current knowledge and research in the field of early childhood education, child development, and related disciplines, as well as on particular knowledge of each child.

Where do you turn to stay informed about research that is designed to inform practice? One place to begin is with NAEYC's revised position statement on developmentally appropriate practice and the most recent edition of *Developmentally Appropriate Practice in Early Childhood Programs Serving Children from Birth through Age 8* (Copple & Bredekamp 2009). In addition, two now-foundational reviews of research published by the National Academy of Sciences—*From Neurons to Neighborhoods* (2000) and *Eager to Learn: Educating our Preschoolers* (2001)—provide an overview and strong foundation that can guide our efforts to base practice on rigorous research.

In addition, NAEYC has many research-based publications and resources that can help you stay abreast of current research and its implications for practice. Two very helpful research-based books are *Informing Our Practice: Useful Research on Young Children's Development* (Essa & Burnham 2009) and *The Intentional Teacher: Choosing the Best Strategies for Young Children's Learning* (Epstein 2007). Every issue of *Young Children*, NAEYC's flagship journal, includes research-based articles, and the journal includes Research in Review, an occasional feature that provides in-depth reviews of research on specific topics. NAEYC also sponsors *Early Childhood Research Quarterly*, a scholarly journal with descriptions of empirical studies addressing issues related to young children and early childhood education, and has links to the NAEYC Center for Applied Research on its website, where you can find research reports and tools for researchers.

The important fact to keep in mind is that best practice is not based on opinions or traditions. It is based on rigorously designed and carefully implemented research that investigates child development and effective teaching. It is our responsibility as early childhood professionals to stay informed about research findings and, to the greatest extent possible, base our practice on this research.

7

Ethical Responsibilities to Community and Society

Early childhood programs operate within the context of their immediate community made up of families and other institutions concerned with children's welfare. Our responsibilities to the community are to provide programs that meet the diverse needs of families, to cooperate with agencies and professions that share the responsibility for children, to assist families in gaining access to those agencies and allied profession-als, and to assist in the development of community programs that are needed but not currently available.

As individuals, we acknowledge our responsibility to provide the best possible programs of care and education for children and to conduct ourselves with honesty and integrity. Because of our specialized exper-tise in early childhood development and education and because the larg-er society shares responsibility for the welfare and protection of young children, we acknowledge a collective obligation to advocate for the best interests of children within early childhood programs and in the larger community and to serve as a voice for young children everywhere.

—NAEYC Code of Ethical Conduct and Statement of Commitment

The fourth and last section of the NAEYC Code of Ethical Conduct spells out early childhood educators' moral obligations to their communities and to society. Most people in our society do not have specialized expertise in child development and early education, so they need to be able to count on those who work in the field to know how to effectively nurture children's development and support their families. The Ethical Responsibilities to Community and Society section reminds us of our individual and collective responsibilities as early childhood educators to use our knowledge to provide accessible and high-quality programs and services for children, to participate in efforts to improve and expand these programs and services, and to take action when those who are responsible for children's welfare do not adequately protect them.

This section addresses early childhood educators' relationship to community and society in two ways. At one level it covers the frequent interactions between early childhood educators and a community's resources and institutions. These involve work with agencies and individuals who evaluate children for special education services; those who investigate suspected child abuse and neglect; and the local library, fire station, and other places that children might visit on learning trips. This section also relates to early childhood educators' commitments to ensure that young children and their families have access to the quality programs and services that they need.

Section IV is the most far-reaching and idealistic portion of the NAEYC Code. It challenges us to take our responsibilities beyond the doors of our classrooms and programs and urges us to be advocates for making the world a better place for young children. One hallmark of a profession is its commitment to a significant social value. In this final section of the Code, we affirm our collective commitment to such a value—the well-being of all children in our society.

This section of the Code was revised in 2005 to make a clear distinction between those ethical responsibilities and guidelines that early childhood educators should follow as individuals and those that we shoulder collectively. While it is true that not all early childhood educators are expected to engage in collective advocacy, it is important that the field as a whole accepts its responsibility to act and advocate on behalf of young children and their families.

Ideals

The Code's eight Ideals relating to community and society outline shared aspirations for providing high-quality education and care programs and services. They call for promoting cooperation and collaboration among all professionals concerned with the welfare of young children. They give direction to our individual and collective efforts to advocate for the well-being of children and their families. And they urge us to strive to further the professional development of the early childhood field and to strengthen the field's commitment to realizing the core values reflected in its code of ethics.

The 2005 revision of the Code differentiated for the first time between early childhood educators' individual and collective ethical responsibilities to community and society. At that time the language of one item (I-4.1) addressing the Ideals of individuals was simplified, and one Ideal addressing our collective responsibility to ensure the implementation of appropriate assessments was added (I-4.5). Five Ideals (I-4.2, I-4.3, I-4.4, I-4.6, I-4.7) were also modified at that time. They better describe our concerns for all children's welfare, address our responsibilities to protect children from violence and to ensure their access to quality programming, and call on early childhood educators to work to change policies and laws that have the potential to put children's well-being at risk. One Ideal (I-4.7) was modified in 2011, reiterating the importance of partnering with families when working to promote policies and laws that protect children. See the chart showing revisions made in 2005 and in 2011 in the Appendix.

Principles

This section's 13 Principles (guides to professional conduct) address early childhood educators' individual and collective obligations to be honest in reporting their qualifications, the services they provide, and the knowledge upon which they base their practice. They direct us to cooperate with other professionals, not hire or recommend for employment persons unsuited for work with young children, and to appropriately respond to unethical or incompetent behavior of colleagues. The Principles call for early childhood educators to be familiar with and abide by laws and regulations that protect children and affirm our collective ethical obligation to protect children's welfare, and to report individuals and programs that violate laws and regulations designed to safeguard children.

Two individual Principles (P-4.5, P-4.7) and one collective Principle (P-4.11) were added during the 2005 revision. One new item explicitly addresses assessment, which was a primary focus of that revision. It calls on individual early childhood educators to be knowledgeable about appropriate assessments and to interpret assessment information accurately for families. The two other new Principles require individuals to be familiar with laws and regulations designed to protect children and to work collectively to change those that do not.

Four Principles relating to individuals (P-4.2, P-4.3, P-4.6, P-4.9) were modified at this time, as was one describing collective responsibilities (P-4.12). Two of these changes address individual responsibilities related to accepting only positions for which we are well qualified and for implementing appropriate hiring practices. Others focus on responsibilities to know and follow appropriate laws and regulations and to report violations of such laws as appropriate, and to follow up with authorities if the situation is not adequately resolved. See the Code Comparison Chart in the Appendix for revisions made in 2005 and in 2011.

Typical ethical dilemmas involving community and society

Although not as many dilemmas relating to community and society were reported in ethics surveys compared to situations relating to families or colleagues, those that were reported dealt with serious issues. They involved violations of licensing regulations and program policies, practices detrimental to children's health and safety, and problems with agencies that are expected to protect children. The section that follows presents three different types of dilemmas that relate to ethical responsibilities to community and society.

Case 12: The staff-child ratio

When Kim accepts a position caring for infants at a child care center, she is unaware of the state's child care regulations on ratios. Once on the job she finds that her work is extremely tiring. After several months at the center, Kim learns that the state requirement is a ratio of no higher than 1:4 for children under 12 months. She works alone in a group that sometimes has as many as seven infants. When the licensing inspector visits, Thelma, the center director, sends the cook to Kim's classroom and leads the inspector to believe that the cook is a teacher who works there regularly.

> What is your first reaction to this situation? To whom does Kim have obligations? What responsibilities should she consider in deciding what she should do? Brainstorm some steps Kim could take to resolve this situation.

What should the ethical early childhood educator do?

A somewhat different version of this situation was published in *Young Children* as part of our original work on ethical dilemmas (Feeney 1987). A similar case was presented recently in the first Focus on Ethics column in *Young Children* (Feeney & Freeman 2011). Some reader responses and analyses from these articles inform the discussion that follows.

Determine the nature of the problem. Kim likes working with babies. She thought that her job would be gratifying, but she is exhausted all the time and worried about what is happening at the center. She calls a friend who also works with infants and toddlers and who went through the early childhood education program with her at a local college. The friend tells her how to locate their state's child care regulations online and tells her about the NAEYC Code of Ethical Conduct.

When Kim reads the Code she begins to understand that she is facing an ethical dilemma. She has a responsibility for the welfare of the children in her group, and she also has a responsibility to be a good employee and to be loyal to her employer. Her feelings are mixed. She wants to do a good job with the babies, but it is difficult with such a large group. She is disappointed in Thelma for not informing her of the state's regulations and, even worse, for lying to the licensing worker. Kim is experiencing a personal conflict as well. She needs her job and fears that expressing her concerns might jeopardize her job security.

This situation involves ethics—Kim is trying to determine whether it would be right to report the licensing infractions or wrong not to report them. When we look at Kim's predicament, we see two possible resolutions, each of which could be justified using the Code (applicable Principles and Ideals are discussed below). The choices are to report the infractions to the licensing agency or to assume that there is a good reason for the director's actions and wait to see if she is planning to address the problem.

Consider ethical finesse. Kim wants very much to find a way to avoid having to choose between her obligations to the children and to her employer. She discusses her situation with the other teachers to learn if they share her concerns and if any of them would like to join her in talking with the director.

Kim and another concerned teacher make an appointment with Thelma. They approach her in a friendly and constructive way, express their concerns, and ask what plans she has for bringing the center into compliance with licensing regulations. Kim's hope is that Thelma has a good explanation for her actions—for example, that she is using the cook to lower the ratios until she receives the results from required background checks she has submitted for a new teacher she wants to hire. If Thelma responds with genuine concern and willingness to improve the situation, Kim plans to delay further action because she doesn't think there is any danger to the children at this point.

If Thelma reduces size of the group and plans to be truthful the next time a licensing inspector comes, this strategy will have successfully resolved the problem. Participants in a workshop discussing this case agreed with this strategy and recommended that that the first thing Kim should do is to communicate her concerns to the director confidentially and respectfully.

Look for guidance in the Code. Thelma appeared to have listened to the teachers' concerns when they talked to her, but she makes no staffing changes at the center. After several weeks of increasing stress, Kim decides that it is time to see how the NAEYC Code can help. In it Kim finds a number of items that help her think about her situation.

She finds no specific guidance in the Core Values, but the Ideals and Principles in the section on Ethical Responsibilities to Children help her understand the seriousness of her obligations to the children. She finds Ideals I-1.4 and I-1.5 especially compelling:

I-1.4—To appreciate the vulnerability of children and their dependence on adults.

I-1.5—To create and maintain safe and healthy settings that foster children's social, emotional, cognitive, and physical development and that respect their dignity and their contributions.

Several Principles are applicable to her situation. As should be done in every situation that affects children's well-being, Kim first considers Principle 1.1:

Above all, we shall not harm children. We shall not participate in practices that are emotionally damaging, physically harmful, disrespectful, degrading, dangerous, exploitative, or intimidating to children.

Kim doesn't think that the teacher-child ratio is directly harmful to the children, but she worries about what could happen if a child were injured or very ill and she had six other children needing her care. She also realizes that the program does not meet Ideal-1.4 in the section of the Code on Ethical Responsibilities to Community and Society:

To provide the community with high-quality early childhood care and education programs and services.

Kim realizes that in speaking to the director in her attempt at ethical finesse, she has already met her ethical responsibilities to coworkers and to her agency:

P-3A.2—When we have concerns about the professional behavior of a coworker, we shall first let that person know of our concern in a way that shows respect for personal dignity and for the diversity to be found among staff members, and then attempt to resolve the matter collegially and in a confidential manner.

P-3B.1—We shall follow all program policies. When we do not agree with program policies, we shall attempt to effect change through constructive action within the organization.

As she continues to study the Code, Kim becomes aware that there are other responsibilities to community and society that are not being addressed by her program, and that she herself is not following the Principles set forth in the Code.

P-4.6—We shall be familiar with laws and regulations that serve to protect the children in our programs and be vigilant in ensuring that these laws and regulations are followed.

P-4.7—When we become aware of a practice or situation that endangers the health, safety, or well-being of children, we have an ethical responsibility to protect children or inform parents and or others who can.

P-4.8—We shall not participate in practices that are in violation of laws and regulations that protect the children in our programs.

Kim tries to balance her responsibilities to her employer and to the children. She considers these items relating to employers.

I-3B.2—To do nothing that diminishes the reputation of the program in which we work unless it is violating laws and regulations designed to protect children or is violating the provisions of this Code.

P-3B.3—We shall not violate laws or regulations designed to protect children and shall take appropriate action consistent with this Code when aware of such violations.

Kim finds in the Code clear guidance about how to begin to address the situation:

P-3B.1—We shall follow all program policies. When we do not agree with program policies, we shall attempt to effect change through constructive action within the organization.

P-3B.5—When we have a concern about circumstances or conditions that impact the quality of care and education within the program, we shall inform the program's administration or, when necessary, other appropriate authorities.

> Have you experienced a work situation in which the program failed to follow laws and regulations designed to protect children? What did you do? Would you, under any circumstances, alert the parents to this violation? Why or why not?

Decide on a course of action. Constructive conversation would be enough to resolve this situation in many real-life situations. But Kim has already attempted constructive action and it has not worked. She now realizes that if children are endangered, the Code provides clear and compelling direction that she must report the problem. The obligation to do no harm to children, as expressed in P-1.1 of the NAEYC Code, is the primary consideration guiding this decision.

Kim knows that she has a moral obligation to act on the children's behalf. She decides to bring the teacher-child ratio concern to the attention of the center's regional office. If she finds no one willing to take action, Kim plans to contact the child care licensing agency in her community. (Reporting a program's violation of state regulations to an appropriate outside authority is referred to as "whistle-blowing.")

Kim also decides that if the ratio in her classroom is not lowered soon, she will look for another place of employment. This is a difficult decision, because she knows that her leaving will have an impact on the children—several infants are just now warming to her, and others who are in a stranger-anxiety stage will not adapt easily to a new caregiver. Even so, Kim does not want to work for a program that she believes does not adequately concern itself with the welfare of children and that violates state regulations and the NAEYC Code of Ethical Conduct.

Policy implications. If the director is responsible for program policy and she has not made it her policy to follow licensing regulations and follow the Code, there is little that can be done in terms of policy. Many programs include the NAEYC Code in their teacher and family handbooks and make it their policy to follow the Code. If that were the case in this program, Thelma would quickly see that she was violating the provisions of the Code and the law and make the necessary changes.

> Do you think Kim is justified in the decision to report violations of licensing regulations? Should any early childhood educator ever work in a program that violates state regulations and conflicts with the NAEYC Code?

Case 13: Misleading the state inspector (a variation of Case 12)

Shana is a teacher in a child development center. The center has some great qualities but is out of compliance with numerous state licensing regulations. Shana is aware that the director sometimes gives incomplete or misleading information about these things to state licensing inspectors. She is struggling to know what to do: is she obligated to report the infractions to an inspector or to the licensing agency? Violations include playground equipment that needs to be repaired, infrequent fire drills, rooms filled beyond their licensed capacity, and failure to maintain required adult-to-child ratios.

We discussed this similar case in the first Focus on Ethics column published in *Young Children* (Feeney & Freeman 2011). It raised many of the same issues as Case 12. Shana, the teacher, went through a similar process of ethical analysis. But Shana decided that if her attempts at ethical finesse—discussing her concerns with the director—did not result in immediate changes, she would have to report the situation to licensing authorities.

The following are four responses we received from readers regarding this scenario:

A child care provider and/or teacher who abides by the NAEYC Code would report the violations listed in this scenario to the licensing agency.

Since the children are at risk due to several issues, including unsafe playground equipment, infrequent fire drill practices, and overcrowding of rooms, Shana should inform appropriate authorities.

If changes are not made, report it to the state agency. Rationale: the Code clarifies expectations of the provider about what is best for the children and what she knows to be legally correct.

Children's safety comes first—P-1.1 in all that we do! She should follow Principle 1.1, and point out relevant items in the Code.

Case 14: The ineffective child protective services agency (Child Abuse Situation III)

Carl is an experienced teacher and aware of his obligations to report suspected child abuse to the local child protective services agency. This responsibility is addressed in the center's policies and procedures manual, consistent with state laws. The last time he made an abuse referral to this agency, however, the caseworker visited the family but did not promptly intervene. The family left town and was not heard from again. Carl is once again facing a potential child abuse situation. He has observed signs of physical abuse to Gloria, a 3-year-old in his group. He has also seen and heard signs that indicate the child's mother may be fearful of the father, who has a quick temper.

This third case concerning reporting of suspected child abuse explores whether the early childhood educator's ethical obligations are different in a situation in which a child protective services agency is known to be ineffective in protecting children.

Situations in which reporting abuse has exacerbated an abuse situation for a child have been reported to us several times. In one case the family removed the child from the program the first time a social worker came to their home to investigate. In another situation, the child was beaten because it was assumed that he had told the teacher about the abuse.

Determine the nature of the problem. Carl has an ethical responsibility and a legal mandate to report the abuse. The ethical dilemma pertains to whether doing so might result in greater harm to the child. The conflicting responsibilities are between his legal and ethical responsibilities and his responsibility to protect a child from harm.

Consider ethical finesse. There is no room for finesse in this situation. A child is endangered and action must be taken immediately.

Look for guidance in the Code. Carl knows that he must report the suspected abuse, although he fears that doing so might result in further injury to the child. He is also aware of the first Principle in the NAEYC Code:

> **P-1.1—Above all, we shall not harm children. We shall not participate in practices that are emotionally damaging, physically harmful, disrespectful, degrading, dangerous, exploitative, or intimidating to children. *This principle has precedence over all others in this Code.***

This Principle is at the root of Carl's dilemma: Following the law to report suspected child abuse could lead to further harm to Gloria.

Carl notes that the following Ideals related to children and community and society are relevant to his predicament:

> I-1.4—To appreciate the vulnerability of children and their dependence on adults.

> I-1.5—To create and maintain safe and healthy settings that foster children's social, emotional, cognitive, and physical development and that respect their dignity and their contributions.

> I-4.7—To support policies and laws that promote the well-being of children and families, and to work to change those that impair their well-being. To participate in developing policies and laws that are needed, and to cooperate with families and other individuals and groups in these efforts.

He finds that these Principles related to individual responsibilities in the section of the Code on Community and Society are also applicable:

> P-4.6—We shall be familiar with laws and regulations that serve to protect the children in our programs and be vigilant in ensuring that these laws and regulations are followed.

> P-4.7—When we become aware of a practice or situation that endangers the health, safety, or well-being of children, we have an ethical responsibility to protect children or inform parents and/or others who can.

> P-4.8—We shall not participate in practices that are in violation of laws and regulations that protect the children in our programs.

He also notices that Collective Principles have been added since he last consulted the Code, and that two of them directly address his situation:

> P-4-12—When we have evidence that an agency that provides services intended to ensure children's well-being is failing to meet its obligations, we acknowledge a collective ethical responsibility to report the problem to appropriate authorities or to the public. We shall be vigilant in our follow-up until the situation is resolved.

P-4.13—When a child protection agency fails to provide adequate protection for abused or neglected children, we acknowledge a collective ethical responsibility to work toward the improvement of these services.

This is a difficult decision. Carl has been a teacher a long time, and he is well aware of his obligation to children's welfare and of the consequences of breaking the law. His greatest fear is that obeying the law might put the child at even more risk.

Decide on a course of action. Carl cannot think of an alternative that is consistent with his legal obligations and might be more effective for protecting the child. He makes the referral. Carl also talks with Beverly, the center director, who is aware of previous instances of reports made to the child protective services agency that were not addressed in a timely manner. Carl and Beverly discuss the problems previously encountered with a supervisor in the child abuse referral unit, and they try to get an assurance that Gloria's case will be handled more effectively. Carl and Beverly follow up the next day by telephone to establish a personal link with the caseworker assigned to work with the family. In P-4.13 the NAEYC Code addresses an early childhood educator's ethical obligations when there is reason to believe that the system doesn't work to benefit children who are abused:

> When a child protection agency fails to provide adequate protection for abused or neglected children, we acknowledge a collective ethical responsibility to work toward the improvement of these services.

After reading this Principle, Carl makes up his mind that if this referral is not handled properly, he will coordinate with Beverly and other concerned staff to alert local child advocacy groups (P-4.12) and work to institute changes in procedures for handling reported child abuse. He will also contact the president of his local AEYC group and his state legislator to discuss ways to improve the protection in their community for children who are victims of abuse. These steps may help to provide adequate protection for children, and the Code reminds us as well of our responsibility "To participate in developing policies and laws that are needed, and to cooperate with families and other individuals and groups in these efforts" (I-4.7).

This case illustrates that early childhood educators do not operate in a vacuum—they are part of a web of community programs and services that are designed to meet children's needs and protect them from harm. It additionally demonstrates that these relationships involve more than making appropriate referrals to community agencies. There is a higher level of obligation to work to ensure these agencies are actually doing an effective job of meeting children's needs.

Share your reaction to Carl's decision. What else could he do to protect the child? What are your obligations when you have reason to believe that following the law might result in harm to a child?

Have you experienced a situation in which a child protective services agency was not effective in protecting children? What actions did you consider or carry out? What was the outcome?

Adult Education Programs and NAEYC Affiliate Groups Can Help Prevent Child Abuse and Neglect

Teacher educators, providers of in-service staff development, and NAEYC Affiliate Groups can make these efforts to help prevent child abuse and neglect:

- Provide preservice and in-service education that includes strategies for supporting families, identifying and responding to the symptoms of abuse and neglect, and interpreting ethical responsibilities to children and families.

- Ensure that people entering the field of early care and education receive training in recognizing the signs of possible child abuse and neglect, following reporting procedures, and understanding and using their code of professional ethics.

- Put the spotlight on public education efforts designed to prevent child abuse and neglect.

- Share websites and publications that offer information on preventing child abuse and neglect.

- Work toward changing laws or regulatory services if they are ineffective in protecting children.

- Participate in developing new laws and regulations that improve conditions for children and work to assure their implementation.

- Influence efforts to improve the child protection services available to children and families.

Case 15: Kindergarten expectations

Malia recently completed a teacher licensure program in early childhood and elementary education. She accepted a job teaching kindergarten in a public school that serves children from families with low incomes, During her teacher licensure program, she especially enjoyed the early childhood coursework and did very well in her student teaching placement, where she demonstrated her skill in implementing integrated curriculum and portfolio assessment. She was dismayed to find that nothing she had learned about appropriate practice and authentic assessment was being implemented in the kindergarten or primary grades in her school. The kindergarten day focused almost exclusively on getting the children ready for a variety of standardized reading and math assessments. Children were stressed and losing their enthusiasm for learning. Some were already viewing themselves as failures because they couldn't meet school expectations. Malia was concerned about the children and disappointed that she couldn't teach and assess children's learning in the ways that had worked so well in her student teaching.

Determine the nature of the problem. We present this last dilemma because we have frequently heard accounts like this from former students who work in schools that emphasize whole-group direct instruction of academic skills and their assessment. Malia and other teachers who work in these kinds of settings need to weigh and balance their responsibilities to children, to families, to their school administrations, and to their community and society. Malia knows that she has an obligation to help children develop skills in reading and math, but she also feels strongly that she has a responsibility to help them leave kindergarten with a positive sense of themselves as learners. She realizes that she is obliged to support the goals and policies of her school, her state department of education, and national education policy. This case presents a complex and thorny dilemma and raises troubling questions about the nature of teaching approaches, curriculum, and assessment in the early grades in the United States at this time.

Consider ethical finesse. Malia knows that as a beginning teacher she is not in a position to change educational practices in her school and that she must follow federal and state mandates. She has studied the NAEYC Code of Ethical Conduct in her college courses and has practiced applying it to many hypothetical situations. She realizes that her best option is to rely on ethical finesse to deal with the problem. She works hard to find ways to incorporate age-appropriate practices into her program. She approaches content standards in creative ways, such as having children make letters with their bodies, counting with real objects, and infusing songs and movement activities into the curriculum. She also tries to do some authentic assessment of children through observation and anecdotal recordkeeping, conversations, and collecting and interpreting work samples. She knows that these practices provide a clearer picture of the children's progress than do paper-and-pencil (or computer-based) tests, but authentic assessment is difficult to do in a group of 25 children when there are so many tests required.

Look for guidance in the Code. Malia is troubled by what she is being required to do in her classroom and what is happening to children in her school. She decides to revisit the NAEYC Code.

She finds two Core Values and many Ideals and Principles that speak to her situation. The most relevant Core Values are the early childhood educator's commitments to

- Appreciate childhood as a unique and valuable stage of the human life cycle, and

- Base our work on knowledge of how children develop and learn.

Many of the Ideals relating to responsibilities to children are pertinent to Malia's situation:

I-1.2—To base program practices upon current knowledge and research in the field of early childhood education, child development, and related disciplines, as well as on particular knowledge of each child.

I-1.3—To recognize and respect the unique qualities, abilities, and potential of each child.

I-1.4—To appreciate the vulnerability of children and their dependence on adults.

I-1.5—To create and maintain safe and healthy settings that foster children's social, emotional, cognitive, and physical development and that respect their dignity and their contributions.

I-1.6—To use assessment instruments and strategies that are appropriate for the children to be assessed, that are used only for the purposes for which they were designed, and that have the potential to benefit children.

I-1.7—To use assessment information to understand and support children's development and learning, to support instruction, and to identify children who may need additional services.

Three Principles relating to children appear to apply to her dilemma:

P-1.1—Above all, we shall not harm children. We shall not participate in practices that are emotionally damaging, physically harmful, disrespectful, degrading, dangerous, exploitative, or intimidating to children. *This principle has precedence over all others in this Code.*

P-1.2—We shall care for and educate children in positive emotional and social environments that are cognitively stimulating . . .

P-1.5—We shall use appropriate assessment systems, which include multiple sources of information, to provide information on children's learning and development.

One Principle relating to ethical responsibilities to employers also has bearing on the situation.

P-3B.1—We shall follow all program policies. When we do not agree with program policies, we shall attempt to effect change through constructive action within the organization.

Malia also finds guidance in Ideals relating to Responsibilities to Community and Society.

I-4.5—To work to ensure that appropriate assessment systems, which include multiple sources of information, are used for purposes that benefit children.

I-4.6—To promote knowledge and understanding of young children and their needs. To work toward greater societal acknowledgment of children's rights and greater social acceptance of responsibility for the well-being of all children.

I-4.7—To support policies and laws that promote the well-being of children and families, and to work to change those that impair their well-being. To participate in developing policies and laws that are needed, and to cooperate with families and other individuals and groups in these efforts.

She is especially struck by one of the collective Principles regarding Community and Society.

P-4.11—When policies are enacted for purposes that do not benefit children, we have a collective responsibility to work to change these policies.

Having completed her review, Malia realizes that many of the teaching approaches and much of the curriculum and testing being implemented in kindergarten and early grade classrooms in her school are unethical according to the NAEYC Code of Ethical Conduct. Malia has been a member of NAEYC since she was a college student and has found the Code very helpful in several situations, but she knows that her administrators and most of the other teachers in her school were not trained in early education and are not aware of it.

Decide on a course of action. Malia realizes that what she is doing in her classroom is better for the children than a steady diet of worksheets or other inappropriate teaching approaches for kindergartners, but still does not provide them with the rich, meaningful experiences in kindergarten that would turn them into excited learners.

She decides to provide other teachers and administrators in her school with information about research on brain development and developmentally appropriate practice. She also expresses her concerns about how much time she is being required to spend assessing children. A few teachers share her reservations, but most of the teachers and administrators don't see anything wrong with the current approach because they are convinced that it is important to demonstrate that the children in the school are meeting required benchmarks.

After two years of teaching, Malia enrolls in a master's program in early childhood education so she can keep up with new literature in the field, and talk with like-minded early childhood educators. She is increasingly frustrated that research on brain development and early learning does not seem to be influencing state or national educational policies, which continue to equate educational quality with scores on standardized tests.

In one of her master's courses, Malia learns about public advocacy and vows to follow the direction of P-4.11of the NAEYC Code and attempt to change school policies. She writes a letter to the editor of the local newspaper and urges others in her school and college classes to write to the paper and submit testimony to the state legislature's education committee regarding early childhood initiatives.

Malia continues to grapple with the feeling that what she is doing isn't right for children. She thinks long and hard about whether she should look for a job in a preschool or private school where she could teach in ways she thinks are better for children. But she cares about the children, and she is recently married and has a young child so she needs the public school salary and benefits to support her family. In the end she decides that she will apply for a transfer to another school in her district that allows teachers more freedom in decision making. Whether or not she gets the transfer, she will stay in the public schools and work in any way she can to effect change for children.

A teacher we know shared these thoughts about how she copes with a situation very much like Malia's. Her words might inspire you if you are facing these same issues in your work:

> I try to keep true to what I believe is important for young children and implement as much of it as I can. It does take a little negotiating, a little give and take on my part. Unfortunately it is a big challenge to bring early childhood practices into a classroom where there are so many mandates and academic expectations. But I've learned that whatever I can do is better than nothing at all. I also find that constant reflection and adjustment helps me to keep things in perspective. I share ideas and knowledge with some teachers at my grade level, and we try to weave in age-appropriate practices wherever we can. Hopefully these practices can grow the more we share with our team of teachers and across grade levels. It is hard to cause change when there are only a few of us, but hopefully we can come together to make change happen and convince others of what is truly important for our young learners.

Policy implications. As this case illustrates, individual teachers rarely can change the view that teaching effectiveness and student achievement should be assessed frequently using standardized tests to compare classrooms and schools rather than for the purpose of improving instruction. At this time in the history of education in the United States, early childhood educators need to work collectively to bring the needs of children back into the awareness of educators and policy makers. We need to make our views heard and help to create new policies that support appropriate teaching approaches, curriculum, and assessment in the early grades. This should be of concern to everyone who works in the field of early childhood care and education. We look forward to a day in the future when all schools for young children focus on the needs and interests of young children and become places for joyful learning.

8

The Code of Ethical Conduct Is a Living Document

Since 1984, when the survey in *Young Children* established that ethics was a serious concern among early childhood educators, NAEYC has done a great deal of work on professional ethics. The core values of the field have been mapped, ethical dilemmas that frequently occur in early childhood settings have been identified, consensus has been reached about how early childhood educators should go about approaching many of these dilemmas, and ethics has been infused into daily practice, teacher education, systems of accreditation, and other Association projects.

NAEYC's Code of Ethical Conduct has become well known and accepted by early childhood educators because it has been widely disseminated and because it is backed by a body of supporting literature that helps practitioners make it a part of their professional repertoire. This book is part of that effort. In our field of early childhood care and education, we can take pride in being in the forefront of the work on professional ethics in education.

Why is a code of ethics important?

The first, and most important, reason why it is vital for early childhood educators to know their code of ethics and build it into their repertoire of professional actions is that the Code is designed to protect children. As pointed out repeatedly in the pages of this book, the first principle in the Code, P-1.1, directs early childhood educators to, above all, refrain from harming children. This powerful statement means that the first priority of every early childhood educator should be the well-being of children, and that every action and decision should first be considered in light of its potential impact on them.

It is valuable for early childhood educators to know about the Code at every career stage. A person entering the field may first encounter professional ethics in a preservice training program. Awareness of the ethical obligations of the early childhood field as spelled out in the NAEYC Code helps the beginner focus on shared values and commitments. It makes it clear that they are not just learning a job—they are joining a community. Learning about professional ethics gives new practitioners a compass to guide them on a path toward ethical conduct in their work. It can also help them to identify the ethical issues they are likely to encounter. Even at the earliest stages of their professional life, novices can begin to use the Code to think through issues involving what is right and wrong, just and unjust, and fair and unfair.

Engagement with professional ethics is important for experienced professionals as well because it can remind them of the shared values of the field, provide a framework for examining their practice more deeply, and raise the level of discussion by enabling intellectually productive dialogue about the issues that they face daily in their work with children and families. Ethics can be the basis of some of professionals' most profound and engaging discussions as they struggle with difficult dilemmas.

The Code of Ethical Conduct and its supplements[1] addressing the particular responsibilities of program administrators and adult educators (faculty members in teacher education programs, trainers, and those who mentor or coach the current workforce) also contribute to the effectiveness of leaders in the field. These position statements give them tools to speak with authority based on the views of the field's largest and most comprehensive professional organization. When informed by these ethical guidelines, leadership is not based solely on personal opinions but reflects the wisdom of the field's commitment to children, families, the workplace, and society.

What makes a code of ethics effective?

Over the years that we have worked on professional ethics in early childhood care and education, we have learned some valuable lessons about what makes a code of ethics useful and effective.

---

[1]These supplements are designed to be used in conjunction with the NAEYC Code; they are not intended to stand alone.

A code is effective when it represents many voices

The members of a profession need to feel that they own their code. The NAEYC Code emerged from the history and traditions of early childhood education in the United States. When developing the Code of Ethical Conduct, NAEYC sought (and has continued to seek) input from grassroots members of the field, both in workshops and through the journal *Young Children*. An important goal was that the development process would be as important as the Code itself. The participative approach that was used for developing the Code was so effective that Kenneth Kipnis, the ethics specialist who helped create the Code, went on to use it in working on code development with other professional groups, including prison doctors and bioethics specialists.

Input from the NAEYC membership has been an important aspect of continuing work on professional ethics. It has been an essential component of revisions of the Code and the development of the supplements to the Code for adult educators and program administrators. The development of the supplements followed the same process as that used for the Code. First, NAEYC convened a workgroup to help identify additional core values, responsibilities, and recurring ethical dilemmas. Then in conference sessions, groups of NAEYC members analyzed cases involving the most prevalent ethical dilemmas. Next, drafts of the supplements inviting comment were published in *Young Children*, posted on the NAEYC website, and presented at conferences. This member feedback was addressed in subsequent drafts of the supplements, and finally the supplements were approved by the NAEYC Governing Board.

A code is effective when it is known and used

Through its activities and supporting literature, NAEYC has made a concerted effort to make the Code available and keep it visible to its membership. More than a million copies of the Code have been printed and distributed in English and Spanish in inexpensive brochures. The Code and its supplements are also available online at www.naeyc.org/positionstatements/ethical_conduct.

Information about professional ethics appears in more than 40 articles in *Young Children*, and in two books on professional ethics published by NAEYC (Feeney et al. 2000; Feeney & Freeman 2012). Beginning in the late 1980s, the journal periodically included articles that solicited members' input in identifying and responding to situations with ethical dimensions. In 2004, *Young Children* and the NAEYC online resource *Beyond the Journal* featured a cluster of articles related to professional ethics in early childhood education. To access an index of abstracts of *Young Children* articles related to professional ethics, go to the journal's page on the NAEYC website, www.naeyc.org/yc.

Information about the history and use of the Code also appears on the NAEYC website in a series of short videos: *Code of Ethical Conduct: Conversations with Stephanie Feeney and Peter Pizzolongo.*

More recently *Young Children* began a regular column, Focus on Ethics. Edited by Stephanie Feeney and Nancy Freeman, the column explores ethical dilemmas submitted by NAEYC members, solicits input from readers, and publishes analyses of each of the cases based on reader input. Three new cases are introduced and debriefed each year. To see published columns, go to www.naeyc.org/yc/columns/focusonethics.

NAEYC national and Affiliate group conferences often include sessions, workshops, and seminars that teach about the Code of Ethical Conduct, illustrate ways to use it, and work through dilemmas that early childhood educators encounter in their work. Some Affiliate groups increase awareness of the Code by providing copies in new member information packets.

The Code of Ethical Conduct is also an integral part of several NAEYC policy documents. The NAEYC Early Childhood Program Standards and Accreditation Criteria include several criteria regarding teaching staff knowing and following ethical guidelines. Guidelines for accreditation of two- and four-year teacher education programs, as well as standards regulating Child Development Associate (CDA) credential programs, mandate inclusion of the Code in the curriculum. These efforts contribute to practitioners' awareness and knowledge of ethical practice as formulated in the Code.

A code is effective when it is revisited regularly

To meet the needs of its members, an organization's code should be revisited regularly to make sure it addresses the current issues and concerns of the field and offers guidance that is relevant for its time. The Code must be responsive to changes in the organization's membership, to the moral climate of our society, and to new challenges faced by practitioners. When the Code was developed, the NAEYC Governing Board decided that it would be regularly reconsidered and revised based on new issues and concerns at the discretion of the executive director of the Association, who schedules periodic review and revision of all position statements to ensure currency and accuracy.

Since 1989, the Code has been revised three times—in 1992, 1997, and 2005. It was reaffirmed and updated in 2011. While the first two revisions were fairly minor, in 2005 nine items were added in response to growing concern over increasingly inappropriate approaches to assessment. The 2005 revision also added one new Core Value: the commitment to "Respect diversity in children, families, and colleagues." And, in recognition of the need for early childhood educators to be effective advocates, new sections on *collective responsibilities* to community and society were added. The 2011 reaffirmation and update of the Code reflects early childhood educators' important responsibilities related to supporting and encouraging family engagement.

We have made great progress in addressing the ethical issues faced by those who work in the early childhood field. The creation of supplements for adult educators and program administrators is another illustration of how work on ethics responds to the needs of various segments of our field. These supplements are designed for groups of early childhood educators whose ethical issues were not specifically addressed in the original Code. Other professional groups who do work related to early childhood education (technical assistance providers, staff in multiservice agencies, and licensing and resource and referral agency staff) also face unique ethical challenges and have indicated interest in exploring the development of additional supplements to the Code to guide their ethical practice.

How can the Code be used?

An article in *Young Children* titled "How Many Ways Can You Think of to Use NAEYC's Code of Ethics?" (NAEYC Ethics Panel 1995) describes a number of ways that programs for children, Affiliate groups, teacher education institutions, and other service agencies have used the Code to support their work with children and families. The article shares strategies that individuals and groups can use to help those who work with young children become aware of and use the Code.

Many uses of the Code presented in that article are now standard practices. In many centers, copies of the Code are routinely distributed to new staff members. Commitment to following the Code is also likely to be included as a part of written staff policies and procedures, and the expectation that every staff member agree to live by the Statement of Commitment is often incorporated into personnel policies. Ethical dilemmas that arise in the workplace and ethics cases in *Young Children* are often discussed in staff meetings. The Code (or a link for it) is also often included in family handbooks so that families are informed about the high standards of practice that guide the program of early care and education to which they have entrusted their children.

Some states require adherence to the NAEYC Code as a licensing criteria. In one state, child care licensing workers distribute copies of NAEYC's Code to centers during their visits. Other states mandate training in ethics and require personnel in licensed centers to have training on the Code and its application annually. The Code is increasingly becoming a part of the preparation of teachers of young children. Descriptions of the Code, its full text, and discussions of professional ethics are included in a growing number of early childhood textbooks. Some teacher education programs give a copy of the Code to all students; others present copies of the Code or the Statement of Commitment that accompanies the Code to new graduates.

The future of ethics in early childhood education

Since 1989, when the Code was adopted, NAEYC has made great progress in making all NAEYC members aware of the moral commitments of early childhood educators and in providing guidance for ethical behavior. But work on ethics in early childhood care and education is far from over. There are many additional actions that could expand upon and strengthen the foundation that already exists. Goals for the future include:

- everyone who cares for young children will turn to the NAEYC Code of Ethical Conduct for guidance when they face troubling ethical situations in their workplace;

- early childhood educators will become ever more skilled in understanding ethics and using the Code—not as an answer book, but as a stimulus for serious reflection about ethical responsibilities;

- all early childhood educators will have a strong sense of identification with the Code and feel that it truly belongs to them;

- everyone who works with young children will have access to consistent and effective training in professional ethics that will help them meet their moral commitments to children and families;

- there will be growing participation in work on ethics, which could include conducting workshops on the Code, involvement in Code revisions, and contributing to the Focus on Ethics column in *Young Children;*

- NAEYC leadership will work to ensure that ethics is prominently included in standards documents, and that provisions are in place to ensure that ethics is adequately addressed;

- early childhood educators will commit themselves to helping others, both within and outside our field, to learn about our moral commitments to children and our Code. We will do this because we know the positive effects of ethical guidance on the welfare of children, and on our sense of competence and professional identity. We took a first step toward this goal when the Association for Childhood Education International (ACEI) endorsed the NAEYC Code and the National Association of Family Child Care (NAFCC) adopted our Code and the two supplements.

- early childhood educators will use our moral commitments to further the collective ideals of seeking a safe world, ensuring high-quality early childhood programs for every child, and becoming ever more skilled in using the Code as a basis for advocating for the needs of young children and their families.

We envision a future in which all early childhood educators honor their commitment to doing what is right; continue to use and disseminate the NAEYC Code; and work together to grow in their understanding of our ethical responsibilities. Work on ethics provides a wonderful opportunity for people from different roles and perspectives to focus on shared values. Attention to professional ethics can strengthen the community of early childhood educators and remind us to keep our moral compasses pointed in the direction of what is best for young children and their families. Making the Code a cornerstone of our professional practice will communicate our dedication to serving young children and their families and will contribute to society's growing appreciation of the increasingly professional workforce caring for and educating America's young children.

The personal and the professional intertwine

Your growth in understanding the Code and your ability to use it with thought and care are ongoing. You will want to consult the Code often to affirm your commitments to children, families, and colleagues; for fortification when you are tempted to do the easiest, but not necessarily the right, thing; and when you need guidance in addressing an ethical dilemma. The Code will support you in doing what is right for young children and their families.

Caring for the youngest, most vulnerable members of our society and being ethical in your practice will have a powerful impact on you. In caring for others and using your expertise on their behalf, you step outside of yourself—and that experience contributes to your sense of being a worthwhile member of society. It brings you back full circle: who you are as a person influences the professional you become, while the professional you become influences who you are as a person.

In the first chapter of this book, we asked you to look at your personal values and morality. In later chapters we urged you to expand your existing values and morality to include the core values and professional guidelines of the early childhood field. In closing, we challenge you to reflect on the interaction of personal values and morality with core values and professional ethics.

You cannot help but be changed by your commitment to doing your work with skill and integrity. Your belief in the importance of working with children may grow stronger with your growing understanding of the lifelong impact of early experiences. Your valuing of children as individuals may mature into advocacy for all children in our society and in the world. Your personal beliefs, values, and morality may be enriched and extended by the core values and ethical precepts of the field of early childhood education.

How do you think your work in early childhood education has affected your personal values and morality? How has the Code influenced your thinking about what is right and wrong in working with young children and their families? Does knowledge of the NAEYC Code of Ethical Conduct change your feelings about the value of the work you do? Has the Code contributed to your sense of being a professional?

References

Bassett, D.L. 2005. Redefining the "public" profession. *Rutgers Law Journal,* Spring.

Bowman, B.T., M.S. Donovan & M.S. Burns, eds. 2001. *Eager to learn: Educating our preschoolers.* Report of the National Research Council, Committee on Early Childhood Pedagogy, Comission on Behavioral and Social Sciences and Education. Washington, DC: National Academy Press.

Cartwright, S. 1999. What makes good early childhood teachers? *Young Children* 54 (4): 4–7.

Chang, H.N. 1999, 2006 revised. Are we supporting diversity? A tool for reflection and dialogue. Work/Family Directions, Inc. & California Tomorrow.

Coady, M. 1991. Ethics, laws and codes. *Australian Journal of Early Childhood* 16 (1): 17–20.

Colker, L.J. 2008. Twelve characteristics of effective early childhood teachers. *Young Children* 63 (2): 68–73. Online: http://www.naeyc.org/files/yc/file/200803/BTJ_Colker.pdf.

Cooper, D. 2003. *Ethics for professionals in a multicultural world.* Upper Saddle River, NJ: Pearson/Prentice Hall.

Copple, C., & S. Bredekamp, eds. 2009. *Developmentally appropriate practice in early childhood programs serving children from birth through age 8.* 3d ed. Washington, DC: NAEYC.

Epstein, A.S. 2007. *The intentional teacher: Choosing the best strategies for young children's learning.* Washington, DC: NAEYC.

Essa, E., & M.M. Burnham, eds. 2009. *Informing our practice: Useful research on young children's development.* Washington, DC: NAEYC.

Feeney, S. 1987. Ethical case studies for NAEYC reader response. *Young Children* 42 (4): 24–25.

Feeney, S. 1995. Professionalism in early childhood teacher education: Focus on ethics. *Journal of Early Childhood Teacher Education* 16 (3): 13–15.

Feeney, S. 2012. *Professionalism in early childhood education: Doing our best for young children.* Englewood Cliffs, NJ: Pearson.

Feeney, S., B. Caldwell & K. Kipnis. 1988. Ethics case studies: The aggressive child. *Young Children* 43 (2): 48–51.

Feeney, S., & R. Chun. 1985. Ethics in review. Effective teachers of young children. *Young Children* 41 (1): 47–52.

Feeney, S., & N. Freeman. 2011. Focus on ethics. The dilemma: Misleading the state inspector. *Young Children* 66 (3): 82–83.

Feeney, S., & N. Freeman. 2012. Focus on ethics. Messy play: The response. *Young Children* 67 (2): 60–64.

Feeney, S., N.K. Freeman & E. Moravcik. 2008. *Teaching the NAEYC code of ethical conduct: Activity sourcebook* (2005 Code Edition). Washington, DC: NAEYC.

Feeney, S., L. Katz & K. Kipnis. 1987. Ethics case studies: The working mother. *Young Children* 43 (1): 16–19.

Feeney, S., & K. Kipnis. 1985. Public policy report and survey. Professional ethics in early childhood education. *Young Children* 40 (3): 54–58.

Feeney, S., S.S. Riley & K. Kipnis. 1988. Ethics case studies: The divorced parents. *Young Children.* 43 (3): 48–51.

Feeney, S., & L. Sysko. 1986. Professional ethics in early childhood education: Survey results. *Young Children* 42 (1): 15–20.

Freeman, N.K., & M.H. Brown. 1996. Ethics instruction for preservice teachers: How are we doing in ECE? *Journal of Early Childhood Teacher Education* 17 (2): 5–18.

Gilligan, C. 1993. *In a different voice: Psychological theory and women's development.* Rev. ed. Cambridge, MA: Harvard University Press.

Gonzalez-Mena, J. 2008. *Diversity in early care and education: Honoring differences.* 5th ed. New York: McGraw-Hill.

Katz, L.G. 1990. On teaching. *Exchange.* January/February: 3–4.

Katz, L.G. 1991. Ethical issues in working with young children. In *Ethical behavior in early childhood education*, Expanded ed., by L.G. Katz & E.H. Ward. Washington DC: NAEYC.

Katz, L.G. 1995. *Talks with teachers of young children.* Norwood, NJ: Ablex.

Katz, L.G., & E. Ward. 1978. *Ethical behavior in early childhood education: A collection.* Washington, DC: NAEYC.

Katz, L.G., & E. Ward. 1991. *Ethical behavior in early childhood education.* Expanded ed. Washington, DC: NAEYC.

Kidder, R.M. 2003. *How good people make tough choices.* Rev. ed. New York: Harper Paperbacks.

Kipnis, K. 1987. How to discuss professional ethics. *Young Children* 42 (4): 26–30.

Kultgen, J. 1988. *Ethics and professionalism.* Philadelphia: University of Pennsylvania Press.

Moran, G. l996. *A grammar of responsibility.* New York: Crossroad Press.

NAEYC. n.d.a. About NAEYC. Online: www.naeyc.org/content/about-naeyc.

NAEYC. n.d.b. NAEYC Mission Statement. Online: www.naeyc.org/about/mission.

NAEYC. 1977. Minutes of the Governing Board meeting. February. Washington, DC: Author.

NAEYC. 1995. How many ways can you think of to use NAEYC's Code of Ethics? *Young Children* 51 (1): 42–43.

NAEYC. 2004. Code of ethical conduct and statement of commitment: Supplement for early childhood adult educators. Washington, DC: Author. Online: www.naeyc.org/files/naeyc/file/positions/ethics04.pdf.

NAEYC. 2005. *Early childhood program standards and accreditation criteria: The mark of quality in early childhood education.* Washington, DC: Author.

NAEYC. 2009. Developmentally appropriate practice in early childhood programs serving children from birth through age 8. Position Statement: Washington, DC: Author. Online: http://www.naeyc.org/files/naeyc/file/positions/PSDAP.pdf.

NAEYC. 2010. Pathways to Cultural Competence Project Program Guide. April. Washington, DC: Author.

NAEYC. 2011. Code of ethical conduct and statement of commitment. Position Statement. Washington, DC: Author. Online: www.naeyc.org/files/naeyc/file/positions/Ethics%20Position%20Statement2011.pdf.

NAEYC Ethics Panel. 1994a. Using NAEYC's code of ethics: A tool for real life. *Young Children* 49 (5): 56–57.

NAEYC Ethics Panel. 1994b. Using NAEYC's code of ethics: A tool for real life. *Young Children* 49 (6): 50–51.

NAEYC Ethics Panel. 1994c. Using NAEYC's code of ethics: A tool for real life. *Young Children* 50 (1): 62–63.

NAEYC Ethics Panel. 1998. What would you do? Real-life ethical problems early childhood professionals face: How do you know if you should suspect child abuse? *Young Children,* 53 (4): 52–54.

Nash, R.J. 2002. *"Real world" ethics: Frameworks for educators and human service professionals.* New York: Teachers College Press.

Noddings, N. 1984. *Caring: A feminine approach to ethics and morality.* Berkeley: University of California Press.

Rodd, J., & M. Clyde. 1991. A code of ethics: Who needs it? *Australian Journal of Early Childhood* 16 (1): 24–34.

Shonkoff, J.P., & D.A. Phillips, eds. 2000. *From neurons to neighborhoods: The science of early childhood development.* Report of the National Research Council and Institute of Medicine. Board on Children, Youth, and Families. Commission on Behavioral and Social Sciences and Education. Washington, DC: National Academy Press.

Stonehouse, A. 1998. *Our code of ethics at work.* Rev. ed., vol. 5, no. 4. AECA Research in Practice Series. Watson, ACT: Australian Early Childhood Association.

Strike, K.A., E.J. Haller & J.F. Soltis. 1988. *The ethics of school administration.* New York: Teachers College Press.

Strike, K.A., & J.F. Soltis. 2009. *The ethics of teaching.* 5th ed. New York: Teachers College Press.

Ungaretti, T., A.G. Dorsey, N.K. Freeman & T.M. Bologna. 1997. A teacher education ethics initiative: A collaborative response to a professional need. *Journal of Teacher Education* 48 (4): 271–80.

Appendix

Code Comparison Chart	
2005	**2011 (changes in bold)**
P-1.3—We shall not participate in practices that discriminate against children by denying benefits, giving special advantages, or excluding them from programs or activities on the basis of their sex, race, national origin, religious beliefs, medical condition, disability, or the marital status/family structure, sexual orientation, or religious beliefs or other affiliations of their families. (Aspects of this principle do not apply in programs that have a lawful mandate to provide services to a particular population of children.)	**P-1.3**—We shall not participate in practices that discriminate against children by denying benefits, giving special advantages, or excluding them from programs or activities on the basis of their sex, race, national origin, **immigration status, preferred home language,** religious beliefs, medical condition, disability, or the marital status/family structure, sexual orientation, or religious beliefs or other affiliations of their families. (Aspects of this principle do not apply in programs that have a lawful mandate to provide services to a particular population of children.)
P-1.4—We shall involve all those with relevant knowledge (including families and staff) in decisions concerning a child, as appropriate, ensuring confidentiality of sensitive information.	**P-1.4**—We shall **use two-way communications to** involve all those with relevant knowledge (including families and staff) in decisions concerning a child, as appropriate, ensuring confidentiality of sensitive information. (See also P-2.4.)
I-2.3—To welcome all family members and encourage them to participate in the program.	**I-2.3**—To welcome all family members and encourage them to participate in the program, **including involvement in shared decision making.**
I-2.5—To respect the dignity and preferences of each family and to make an effort to learn about its structure, culture, language, customs, and beliefs.	**I-2.5**—To respect the dignity and preferences of each family and to make an effort to learn about its structure, culture, language, customs, and beliefs **to ensure a culturally consistent environment for all children and families.**
I-2.8—To help family members enhance their understanding of their children and support the continuing development of their skills as parents.	**I-2.8**—To help family members enhance their understanding of their children, **as staff are enhancing their understanding of each child through communications with families,** and support family members in the continuing development of their skills as parents.

2005	Code—2011 (changes in bold)
I-2.9—To participate in building support networks for families by providing them with opportunities to interact with program staff, other families, community resources, and professional services.	**I-2.9—To foster families' efforts to build** support networks **and, when needed,** participate in building networks for families by providing them with opportunities to interact with program staff, other families, community resources, and professional services.
P-2.2—We shall inform families of program philosophy, policies, curriculum, assessment system, and personnel qualifications, and explain why we teach as we do—which should be in accordance with our ethical responsibilities to children (see Section I).	P-2.2—We shall inform families of program philosophy, policies, curriculum, assessment system, **cultural practices,** and personnel qualifications, and explain why we teach as we do—which should be in accordance with our ethical responsibilities to children (see Section I).
P-2.4—We shall involve the family in significant decisions affecting their child.	P-2.4—We shall **ensure that the family is involved** in significant decisions affecting their child. (See also P-1.4.)
P-2.6—As families share information with us about their children and families, we shall consider this information to plan and implement the program.	P-2.6—As families share information with us about their children and families, we shall **ensure that families' input is an important contribution** to the planning and implementation of the program.
I-4.7—To support policies and laws that promote the well-being of children and families, and to work to change those that impair their well-being. To participate in developing policies and laws that are needed, and to cooperate with other individuals and groups in these efforts	I-4.7—To support policies and laws that promote the well-being of children and families, and to work to change those that impair their well-being. To participate in developing policies and laws that are needed, and to cooperate **with families** and other individuals and groups in these efforts.

Section III-C: Ethical Responsibilities to Employees from the 2005 version of the Code was deleted in 2011, as these Ideals and Principles are included in the reaffirmed and updated Supplement for Early Childhood Program Administrators (2011).

Recommended Reading

We hope that this book has demonstrated how important it is for early childhood educators to understand their moral commitments and to know and use the NAEYC Code of Ethical Conduct. We also hope that it has kindled in you an interest in learning more about ethics and professionalism. Following is a list of books that may be helpful if you wish to learn more about these topics:

Books

Ayers, W. 2005. *Teaching toward freedom: Moral commitment and ethical action in the classroom.* Boston: Beacon Press.
 Describes education as an undertaking that can help students become more fully human, more engaged, and more free.

Feeney, S. 2012. *Professionalism in early childhood education: Doing our best for young children.* Englewood Cliffs, NJ. Pearson.
 Addresses what it means to be a professional and considers the professional status and prospects of early childhood education.

Feeney, S., N.K. Freeman & E. Moravcik. 2008. *Teaching the NAEYC Code of Ethical Conduct: Activity sourcebook* (2005 Code Edition). Washington, DC: NAEYC.
 This companion to *Ethics and the Early Childhood Educator* offers engaging ways to introduce college students and teachers to the NAEYC Code of Ethical Conduct and provides them opportunities to practice its application.

Gardner, H.E., M. Csikzentmihalyi & W. Damon. 2002. *Good work: When excellence and ethics meet.* New York: Basic Books.
 Investigates two professions, genetics and journalism, striving under pressure to do excellent work that still benefits society.

Gilligan, C. 1982. *In a different voice: Psychological theory and women's development.* Cambridge, MA: Harvard University Press.
 Presents a description of women's moral development. This is a foundational resource.

Goffin, S.G. & V. Washington. 2007. *Ready or not: Leadership choices in early care and education.* New York: Teachers College Press.
 Calls on early childhood educators to reflect on issues of purpose, identity, and responsibility in the early childhood field.

Gonzalez-Mena, J. 2008. *Diversity in early care and education: Honoring differences,* 5th ed. New York: McGraw-Hill.
Emphasizes the importance of working effectively with culturally diverse children and families and provides strategies to effectively incorporate diverse perspectives into early care and education settings.

Kagan, S.L., K. Kauerz & K. Tarrant. 2008. *The early care and education teaching workforce at the fulcrum.* New York: Teachers College Press.
Synthesizes research on the early care and education workforce and explores issues including teacher quality, teacher effectiveness, and professional development.

Katz, L.G. 1995. *Talks with teachers of young children: A collection.* Norwood, NJ: Ablex.
Foundational essays, originally published between 1977 and 1985, that paved the way for much of the current work on ethics in early childhood education. See particularly Chapter 11, The professional preschool teacher; Chapter 14, The nature of professions: Where is early childhood education; and Chapter 15, Ethical issues in working with young children.

Kidder, R.M. 2003. Rev. ed. *How good people make tough choices: Resolving the dilemmas of ethical living.* New York: Harper Paperbacks.
Introduces the study of ethics and ethical decision making in a clear, easy-to-read manner. This is a good place to begin your further study of ethics.

Kultgen, J. 1988. *Ethics and professionalism.* Philadelphia: University of Pennsylvania Press.
Explores the connection between morality and professional ideals, examines the structure and organization of occupations and the ideals and ideology of professions.

Lawrence-Lightfoot, S. 2000. *Respect: An exploration.* Perseus Books.
Explores the empowering nature of respect in the relationship between a helping person and the person being helped.

Lawrence-Lightfoot, S. 2003. *The essential conversations: What parents and teachers can learn from each other.* New York: Random House Publishing
Examines the crucial exchange that occurs between parents and teachers—the dialogue between the most important people in a child's life.

Nash, R.J. 2002. *"Real world" ethics: Frameworks for educators and human service professionals.* New York: Teachers College Press.
Considers how those in the service professions approach ethical dilemmas by melding their personal morality and character with professional ethics to guide their efforts at problem solving.

Noddings, N. 1984. *Caring: A feminine approach to ethics and moral education.* Berkeley: University of California Press.
Explores characteristics of the caring relationships that lie at the heart of work with young children and their families. This is a foundational work.

Strike, K.A., & J.F. Soltis. 2009. *The ethics of teaching.* 5th ed. New York: Teachers College Press.
Applies ethical theories to teachers' work and presents a model of ethical decision making. A basic resource for examining ethical issues in education.

Wineberg, T.W. 2008. *Professional care and vocation: Cultivating ethical sensibilities in teaching.* (Professional Learning. Vol. 5.) Rotterdam/Taipei: Sense Publishers.
Integrates the traditional understanding of a profession (a calling to selfless service) with that of vocation (work that offers a deep sense of personal fulfillment, meaning, and identity).

Online resources

Halgunseth, L.C., A. Peterson, D.R. Stark & S. Moodie. 2009. *Family engagement, diverse families, and early childhood education programs: An integrated review of the literature.* Washington, DC: NAEYC, The Pew Charitable Trusts. Online: http://www.naeyc.org/files/naeyc/file/research/FamEngage.pdf
Presents an overview of research on family engagement in early childhood education, emphasizing successful ways early childhood educators can partner with families to benefit children.

NAEYC Publications that Address Professional Ethics
http://www.naeyc.org/files/naeyc/file/ecprofessional/Ethics%20Resources%20Bibliography%20Final%2003-10(1).pdf

NAEYC. 2004. Code of ethical conduct: Supplement for early childhood adult educators. Washington, DC: Author. Online: www.naeyc.org/files/naeyc/file/positions/ethics04.pdf.

NAEYC. 2011. Code of ethical conduct: Supplement for early childhood program administrators. Washington, DC: Author. Online: www.naeyc.org/files/naeyc/file/positions/Supplement%20PS2011.pdf.

About the Authors

Stephanie Feeney is professor emerita of education at the University of Hawaii at Manoa, where she directed undergraduate and graduate early childhood education programs for many years. She received her bachelor's degree at UCLA, master's at Harvard University, and Ph.D. at Claremont Graduate University.

Professor Feeney is a former member of the NAEYC Governing Board and has participated in all of NAEYC's efforts related to professional ethics. She is coauthor with Professor Kenneth Kipnis of the original NAEYC Code of Ethical Conduct and has been involved in all of the subsequent revisions of the Code. She was an active participant in the development of the Supplement to the Code of Ethical Conduct for Adult Educators and the Supplement to the Code for Early Childhood Program Administrators. She is coeditor of Focus on Ethics, a regular feature in *Young Children,* and co-led NAEYC's online Q&A on Ethics.

Professor Feeney has served several terms on the Board of the National Association for Early Childhood Teacher Educators (NAECTE) and the Hawaii AEYC. She is author of *Professionalism in Early Childhood Education: Doing Our Best for Young Children* and *Early Childhood Education in Asia and the Pacific.* She is coauthor of *Who Am I in the Lives of Children?* (9th ed.), *Meaningful Curriculum for Young Children, Continuing Issues in Early Childhood Education* (3d ed.), and *Teaching the NAEYC Code of Ethical Conduct.* She has written and presented widely about social studies for young children, children's literature, ethics, and professionalism. She has also coauthored a curriculum for young children and written four children's books about Hawaii.

Nancy K. Freeman is an associate professor of early childhood education and director of the Yvonne and Schuler Moore Child Development Research Center at the University of South Carolina in Columbia, where she teachers graduate and undergraduate courses and oversees and facilitates research activities and university students' placements at its Children's Center. She received her bachelor's degree from St. Mary's College of Notre Dame, Indiana, and completed her master's and Ph.D. at the University of South Carolina.

Dr. Freeman has actively participated in workgroups revising NAEYC's Code of Ethical Conduct and in the development of the Supplements to the Code of Ethical Conduct for Adult Educators and for Early Childhood Program Administrators. She is coeditor of Focus on Ethics, a regular feature in *Young Children,* and co-led NAEYC's online Q&A on Ethics.

Dr. Freeman is past president of the National Association for Early Childhood Teacher Educators (NAECTE) and has served on its Board for many years. She has been active in NAEYC at the state and national levels and was honored by South Carolina's NAEYC Affiliate for her leadership and contributions. She also chairs South Carolina's Governor's Committee on the Regulation of Child Care Facilities.

Dr. Freeman is coauthor of *Teaching the NAEYC Code of Ethical Conduct* and *Administration of Early Childhood Education* (10th ed.). She has also written and presented widely on professional ethics, service learning, play, and teacher education.

Peter J. Pizzolongo is associate executive director at the National Association for the Education of Young Children. He has over 35 years' experience as an author, training and technical assistance provider, teacher educator, program evaluator, Head Start and child care agency administrator, human services program manager, and early childhood education specialist. Mr. Pizzolongo has authored or coauthored more than 30 publications, online and video programs, and other resources. He served as staff liaison to the NAEYC Governing Board-appointed workgroup for the 2005 revision of the Code of Ethical Conduct and Statement of Commitment and staffed the 2011 update of the Code.